BILLION DOLLAR TURNAROUND

THE 3M SPINOFF THAT BECAME IMATION

About the Author

William T. Monahan spent his entire business career with 3M Corporation and Imation, a spinoff of 3M. He began work in 1972 as a sales rep in New York City and progressed through a number of marketing and management positions. He ran 3M businesses in Europe and worldwide, and led the Data Storage Division, the Italian subsidiary, and the Austin, Texas, group of divisions in the Electronic, Telecommunications, and Electrical businesses.

As Imation's newly-appointed CEO, Bill formed that business during the period beginning in late 1995 through the first six months of 1996. Imation's spinoff as a separate public company officially became effective on July 1, 1996, and his term as Imation's chief executive continued until he retired in May 2004.

Bill and his wife of 34 years, Linda, have two children, William Junior and Kelly, and three grandchildren, all living in the West Chester, Pennsylvania area.

BILLION DOLLAR TURNAROUND

THE 3M SPINOFF THAT BECAME IMATION

BY

WILLIAM T. MONAHAN

RICHMOND, VIRGINIA

First Edition

ISBN 1-892538-22-9

If your bookseller does not have this book in stock,
it can be ordered directly from the publisher.
Contact us for information about discounts
on quantity purchases.

The Oaklea Press
6912 Three Chopt Road, Suite B
Richmond, Virginia 23226

Voice: 1-800-295-4066
Facsimile: 1-804-281-5686
Email: Info@OakleaPress.com

This book can be purchased online at
http://www.LeanTransformation.com

Imation and the Imation logo are trademarks of Imation Corporation. 3M and the 3M logo are trademarks of The 3M Company.

Dust jacket designed by Stephen Brandt.

Dedication

I dedicate this book to my wife, Linda,
without whose sacrifice, love, support
and capability I could not have had
a career or a family

and to

the employees of Imation, the people
all over the world who had the courage
and dedication to stay the course though
the tough times and build a successful,
sustainable company.

CONTENTS

Introduction

How do you create a successful, thriving company out of a motley collection of business units that are performing anemically at best, or at worst, losing money? Perhaps you are the CEO of a public company who is considering spining off part of it so you can concentrate on your core business. Maybe you've just been put in charge of a business that's struggling. Or maybe you're the leader, or one of an executive team that's going through hard times, and the only way to glimpse the light at the end of the tunnel is through drastic change. The intent of this book is to provide helpful guidance.

Imation Corporation began as a spinoff from 3M, the highly-respected Midwestern company and manufacturer of such well-known brands as Scotch® tape and Post-it® notes. The decision by 3M management to spin off the units that became Imation was smart. By shedding business units that were a drag on 3M, the value of the company's stock was enhanced, thereby creating shareholder value. Seven low-profit or unprofitable and, for the most part, unrelated businesses were let go. These were businesses that no longer fit 3M's model—a model that had worked extremely well for 3M over the years. The units had become a serious drag on the company's profitable portfolio because it was virtually impossible for them to make profit as long as they operated under the 3M business formula. They'd caused numerous migraines for the managers responsible because time and effort had been spent year in and year out trying to "fix" them—time and effort 3M management came to believe could be spent more productively on other, better opportunities.

As will be shown, the evolution of the businesses, including technology, competition and markets served, was different than what could be found at the rest of 3M. The cost and pricing structures they would require to be successful were considerably different than what 3M was accustomed to, and virtually impossible to achieve under 3M's corporate structure at that time. Of course, this did not mean it wasn't possible for the businesses to make a profit and be competitive under the right circumstances. Nevertheless, recognizing the situation clearly and dispassionately was an important first step.

The solution was drastic change. The businesses had to be led through a wrenching transformation in order to fit a new and different business model. Making this happen wasn't easy, but coupled with strict financial discipline and stringent adherence to business fundamentals, the changes led to a one-billion-dollar cash turnaround, and the creation of a profitable and sustainable company from what had been a mix of business units in peril.

Join me as we look back at the period from the end of 1995 through 2004. You are about to witness a profound turnaround brought about by excellent people, realignment of cost structures, the institution of a new and dynamic corporate culture, the use of effective new decision-making and negotiation techniques, and the adoption of a focused portfolio strategy. You'll see how divestitures and alignment of investment priorities brought needed cash into the business. And perhaps the most important single factor of all, you'll see how Imation has evolved into a successful, ongoing and sustainable business today because of the focus placed on the financial implications of decisions made during those formative years.

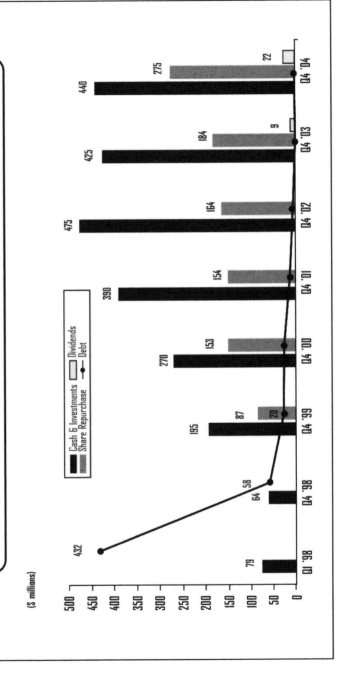

Financial Condition

A financial turnaround of $1 billion has been achieved since first quarter 1998

($ millions)

Legend: Cash & Investments | Dividends | Share Repurchase | Debt

Quarter	Cash & Investments	Share Repurchase	Dividends	Debt
Q1 '98	79			432
Q4 '98	64			58
Q4 '99	195	87	20	
Q4 '00	270	153		
Q4 '01	390	154		
Q4 '02	475	164		
Q4 '03	425	184	9	
Q4 '04	440	275	22	

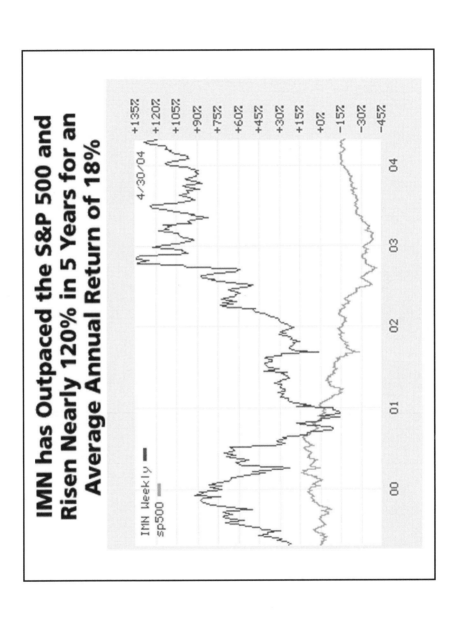

IMN has Outpaced the S&P 500 and Risen Nearly 120% in 5 Years for an Average Annual Return of 18%

Chapter One: How It All Began

In November, 1995, about Midnight in Taiwan, my involvement in the spinoff began. The next day I was scheduled to return to the States after a three-week business trip through Asia. I was in a hotel room, sound asleep, when the telephone rang. My boss, Larry Eaton, was on the line. He let me in on what was perhaps the biggest and best-kept secret in 3M's history. The announcement would come on Monday. Seven businesses in his sector were being spun off. But what he said next really woke me up. You see, I was running 3M's business group in Austin, Texas. The CEO, Livio D. DeSimone, or "Desi," was in St. Paul at 3M headquarters. Larry said Desi might stop by to see me.

"Really?" I said. " Is he coming to Austin?"

"No, no," he said. "You're going to St. Paul."

That's how it began.

I was familiar with most of the businesses involved in the spin, and in fact had run Data Storage for more than six years. My career had been marked by my involvement in successful turnarounds for 3M, first in Europe for Data Storage, then for all of Data Storage internationally, and finally, in 1986, the entire Data Storage Division. After that, I'd been sent to Italy to run all 3M businesses there. Italy was where I'd come into contact with the Imaging businesses in the spinoff.

Since I'd been successful in turning distressed businesses around, I suppose I was seen as someone to put in charge when dramatic change was needed. That was why I'd been pulled back from Italy and sent to Austin. The five divisions of 3M there were not doing as well as in the past. Now, after making some tough changes, things were moving along fine.

So that's where I was, running a group totally unrelated to what was being spun off, business units in the same sector, but not the same group. I suppose, due to my reputation, the leaders of 3M hoped the people being cut loose from 3M in the spin would feel better about what was happening if I took the job. I knew many of the executives involved, as well as the businesses. And they knew me.

So I went to St. Paul, and the CEO offered me the job.

I took a weekend and thought about it. Should I, or shouldn't I? As you can imagine, it was an intense few days. I'd spent my whole career at 3M. I was in a good position. The businesses I was running were doing very well. But I knew the spinoff businesses were in for very tough financial challenges. Some, like Data Storage and Medical Imaging, were losing money and were heavily invested in new technology that hadn't yet been launched. Other businesses like Printing & Publishing and Photo Film were making money but facing futures in industries moving quickly from analog to digital technology and shrinking gross margins.

Photo Film was one I knew well because it was based in Italy, and I'd been involved with it when I was there. The unit had a huge and costly infrastructure to support. It's position was already small in a market that was shrinking fast. Fuji and Kodak offered stiff competition. It was a private label business with a bleak outlook because, perhaps more ominous than anything else, digital was coming on strong. It seemed apparent it was only a matter of time before this business would have to be sold or closed.

As far as the other businesses in the spin were concerned, margins were constantly being squeezed and could be expected to continue on a steady decline. Plus, they had other troubles facing them. Mainly, they were in a state of profound transition, caught up in the change from the material science world—in which 3M had long been a mover and shaker—to the fast-moving new digital business environment characterized by rapid change and aggressive price competition. What 3M was doing made a great deal of sense—for 3M. Shedding these businesses would enhance 3M's stock value and free top executives to concentrate on units that conformed to the 3M business model. But it was far from certain if the new company could survive on its own.

There was no doubt about it. Newco, as it was called originally, faced difficult financial and business challenges. Here was a collection of businesses with little or no market synergy. The company had more than 12,000 employees worldwide, a large percentage of whom were staff and administration as dictated by 3M's corporate model. Sales, general and administrative (SG&A) costs were nearly thirty percent of sales, which was totally unaffordable if the company was to survive in the competitive, low gross margin business arenas of the units that made up the new company. On top of all this, change of any kind brings uncertainty and fear and this meant customers would also be nervous and watching closely what was going on as 3M cut these units loose.

The Decision to Take the Job

What should I do? I knew my future was secure at 3M. I'd been on a fast track. The businesses I was running were exciting and successful.

As always, my wife, Linda, was my biggest supporter and ally. She was ready and confident to take it on if that's what I wanted, and what we agreed was best. I also spoke to my father, a conservative business man who'd always been a key mentor for me, who had succeeded in very tough businesses.

We'd have to move back to St. Paul, but relocating was not a big issue. I knew if I stayed at 3M we'd likely be back there anyway in the next few years. Even though this would be our sixth move, Linda and I both thrived on change.

The truth is, it didn't take long to realize I couldn't turn down this challenge. It was a once in a lifetime opportunity. And, as it turned out, I believe I learned and experienced more as the CEO of Imation—forming it, changing it, leading it—than I ever could have if I'd stayed at 3M—even if I'd become CEO.

In making the decision, my thought process was simple. I'd done turnarounds at 3M almost my entire career. I'd been in some really tough business situations, and the truth is, I'd thrived on them. This was the ultimate turnaround challenge.

As a matter of background, 3M had moved my family all over the world and the country and, fortunately, my wife liked new adventures. She handled challenges very well, and could operate on her own. We had moved from New York to Minnesota, then to Brussels and back, then to Italy, and finally to Texas. She'd always been up to the change and had made the moves work for our family. The longest we'd ever lived in one place was a nine year period in Minnesota, between Brussels and Italy, and during that time we had changed towns three times.

In my experience as an executive, I've observed an important fact about relocating people. Careers are often built and survive as a result of the partnership of a family. Many solid careers, and particularly successful foreign assignments, are the result of partnerships with strong, supportive and independent spouses who can handle the unknown and deal with changes on their own. In effect, the spouse of an executive holds the family together while a career is established through a series of challenging assignments. My conclusion is that it would be very difficult, almost impossible, perhaps, to have a successful international career and a family without a spouse who partners to help make it happen.

Don't Pass Up an Opportunity

Some people think you can ruin your career if you turn down a promotion that requires you to move, but I have to say, that's not necessarily so, though you may get the person who offered you the job miffed at you. That may be one reason I never believed in having just one mentor or sponsor. I developed plenty of contacts. If you network widely, you can usually overcome a touchy situation.

Even so, I believe moving around a lot paid off for me. International, for example, helped me get to know people in influential positions throughout the company. It was a big boost to my career. It's a simple fact of life that when you're outside of the country, you meet higher level people than you meet when you have a mid-level job at headquarters. You are usually in a make or break assignment due to the visibility of the position you hold, but this offers a real opportunity for advancement. So, you might say the upside is as great or greater than the downside.

I did not take every opportunity that came down the pike. While I was working in Data Storage I had offers from 3M executives that would have taken me out of that very challenging business. However, I believed in the future of the Data Storage business and I wanted to be part of its turnaround.

An example of this was when I was offered the job of Managing Director of Chile. The President of 3M International knew me well and saw the International business I ran for Data Storage was doing well while domestically the business was struggling. He wanted to give me a chance to get out of Data Storage and into a more stable area. I believe he felt he was doing me a favor, saving me from a potential losing situation, by putting me in a coveted role in Chile.

At first, I didn't know what to do. I didn't want to leave Data Storage. Changes were badly needed, but I believed I could be part of the successful change the business required. What it came down to was that I wasn't interested in leaving Data, and my wife, in that instance, wasn't gung ho about going to Chile. Linda had always had a part in any change decision. If she wasn't in favor of something, I wasn't going to force the family to do it.

So I turned down the job. The President challenged me on it.

He came to see me and he said, "I didn't just ask you to go to Chile, I want you to go." This was the International President, and one of the two most powerful people in the company.

I still said, "No."

But the fact is, it never hurt me. I ended up running all of Data Storage. I realize some people thought I was nuts to stay. But the challenge of turning around a business I was committed to was much too attractive, and there was something else. The people who made up that business were excellent and they deserved my loyalty.

Now, the ultimate challenge had been presented to me for the taking—a group of businesses totaling $2.4 billion in sales badly in need of change and a turnaround. It was a career-defining challenge that could not be passed on.

Cut Adrift From 3M

It hit people like a baseball bat. The day of the announcement, you weren't a 3Mer any more. Whether you were spun off, or volunteered, you were part of a group apart. Oh, you still went to managers' meetings, but it was clear you were no longer part of 3M. We were cohabiting, but that was all. Once it was clear the unit you worked for was being cut loose, you were an outsider even though it wouldn't be official for seven months.

A lot of good people wished us well but only a few executives really stepped up to support the formation of a new company. Many who were not going with the spinoff were concerned the new company would get more from 3M than they thought it should. It quickly became "us versus them" with the "them" holding most of the cards.

The atmosphere was thick. With only a few exceptions, the management teams who headed the new entity felt betrayed by 3M. Like most in the higher levels of 3M, they had long labored under the assumption they held secure positions and could count on lifetime employment. For these folks, the spinoff announcement came like a lightning bolt out of a bright blue sky. Many of the rank and file were also frightened, uncertain, and concerned about their livelihoods. They, too, were bitterly disappointed at being "thrown out" of 3M. Yet it was clear to me the new company could survive only if those who comprised it were personally committed to success.

No wonder people were skittish. Rather than being included in the spin, the video cassette business (VHS tapes) was closed down. Closing a business was not something 3M had been accustomed to doing. But no company that manufactured these tapes was making very much money on them because of over capacity in the industry, the result of which was ridiculously low prices. So, rather than spin it off, 3M closed it. This, and the spinoff of the other divisions, combined for a real shocker. The concept that 3M offered lifetime employment ended on that day, not only for the 12,000 people who were spun off, but for those who remained. Before then, people had never thought 3M would do such a thing. The realities of business in a global economy had dawned at 3M in November, 1995.

So we had customers, management and employees who were looking cautiously over their shoulders. On top of this, it was pretty certain we were going to lose almost all our shareholders. The way the deal worked, a 3M shareholder would get one share of Imation for every ten 3M shares owned, making this a tax free spin off. The idea was to create wealth for the shareholders. But it was a foregone conclusion most 3M shareholders wouldn't want to hold Imation. 3M was an established company that had performed well year after year. It paid a handsome dividend and was a safe place to put one's money. Holding the stock made perfect sense for long-term investors and pension funds. As a start up, however, Newco wasn't going to pay a dividend. Besides this, the new company was in the volatile high-tech digital arena. It was a speculative stock— not the sort the typical 3M shareholder would want to buy or to own. There also were institutional investors who could not, because of their by-laws, hold Imation stock as we would not be paying a dividend. It seemed obvious that over a period of time, perhaps a year, we were going to have to replace all or most of our shareholders. So there we were, in what was a shaky situation at best. From the outset, it was clear change would have to come quickly if Newco was to survive.

Why I Took the Challenge

I've been asked many times why I took such a high-risk job. The answer is simple. It was a chance to implement my vision of what a company could be. Decision making would be streamlined, I believed in pay-for-performance, in eliminating what I considered to be communistic pay practices, and in developing a true customer focus. Finance would become the center of the business. Plus, with a fresh start, unproductive decisions which had been made in the past could be undone. It was an opportunity that rarely comes along, so it didn't take me long to decide. The only kicker was, it proved to be more challenging than I ever could have dreamed, and I had to learn on the job. I was not yet prepared for this level of challenge and I knew I had to learn fast and get good people very engaged if we were to survive and win.

LESSONS LEARNED:

- Don't turn down a challenging opportunity. If you think you have the talent and what it takes to get the job done, step up to it.

- Your spouse and family must be as committed as you are.

- When you are part of a spinoff, you're an outsider the day the spinoff is announced. Be realistic and deal with it.

- There's no such thing as job security in today's global marketplace. Every company must compete and streamline to succeed.

- You are only as good as the talent around you. Get the leadership right first!

Chapter Two: The First Seven Months

3M is one of the biggest employers, and one of the most respected companies headquartered in Minneapolis-St. Paul. The spinoff announcement was huge, and it came as a shock to many that this company would spin off a half-dozen or so of its businesses into an separate public entity. The news hit the local papers in a big way. Stories appeared on public radio, in the newspapers, magazines, and in business publications.

Only a handful of people knew anything before the announcement. The spin had been put together by a few top executives at 3M, and the board of directors, along with the help of outside consultants. No one in the businesses to be spun was involved except Larry Eaton, who headed the sector they were part of. Bain & Company, a management consulting firm out of Boston was one of the architects. The firm did a good job and was a help to us before and after the spin took place. Their influence had a lot to do with our strategy to focus on and build our core value.

3M had made a few acquisitions over the years, but had seldom gone through major divestitures. They were now divesting almost seventeen percent of the company. This was positioned as a strategic move to enable 3M to get back to their core. The goal of the company was to focus on what they did well, rather than on businesses that were headed off into what at that time was the unknown world of digital.

Given a choice, however, 3M might not have spun off

Data Storage. It fit well with a number of the other 3M distribution businesses. When I had run Data Storage earlier in my career, our team built sales of $170 million through the office market division of 3M. All that went away in the spin. But the spin was not viable without Data, so 3M had to include it.

The people who were most shocked were those who thought they had an unwritten lifetime deal with 3M. To their shock, the promise of lifetime employment no longer existed. Employees of the businesses to be spun would no longer be 3Mers. This was sixteen or seventeen percent of 3M's employees and sales, no small number. But 3M was doing what it had to do and what it believed to be best for both companies. The alternatives were not positive. It would have been necessary to close some businesses and downsize the others, and the spinning eliminated the human resources issues 3M would otherwise have had to deal with. It's helpful to understand that 3M's image was a huge asset and important to management. Up to this time, the company had seldom gone though downsizing. In the past, if cutting staff was necessary, the people involved were put on an unassigned list and given six months to find another assignment within 3M. This is why there weren't many cuts in the seven months between the announcement and the official spinoff. Employees who were being spun off felt betrayed. They were very concerned about their personal situations, and about the future of the new company without 3M's support.

The businesses spun off were in the fields of Medical Imaging, Printing & Publishing, Data Storage, CD Rom

Duplication, Photo Film, Break-Fix services related to Medical and Printing, and Engineering Systems. (See Appendix for descriptions of the businesses.)

The Data Storage and Information Management business was a worldwide leader in developing and manufacturing a full line of removable data storage products to help customers manage, store and share data for the desktop and mobile, network and data center environments. The unit had more than three hundred technology scientists and more than three hundred data storage patents in the United States alone. The other businesses included the world's leading supplier of color proofing materials for the graphic arts industry, as well as a strong position in printing plates. The Medical Imaging business was a leading supplier of laser imagers for medical diagnostics, with unique dry film technology about to be introduced. This unit also was a supplier of conventional X-ray films. Also included in the spin was a private-label color photography film business for the consumer market, a microfilm document management business, an imaging equipment services business, a CD replication business and a carbonless paper business. About the only things these businesses all had in common was that they came from 3M, and they were in low-margin markets with high investment costs and increasing price pressure—usually exerted by large Japanese competitors. As valued as the 3M culture and heritage were, the units needed a new business model that focused on their core competencies and enabled them to respond quickly to fast-changing digital technologies and competitive markets. They needed lower operating costs and a lean corporate structure. In other words, big changes were ahead for the business units of this new company if it was to survive.

We Get Off to a Fast Start

After the spinoff announcement we hit the ground running. Between November 1995, and July 1, 1996 we had to create an all-new public company with all the documentation and legal requirements in place. We couldn't do any broad restructuring before the launch because 3M had veto power and wanted a smooth, non-controversial launch. 3M preferred all the HR issues be on our watch, not theirs. This was, after all, one of the major reasons for the spin. We did close some plants, and we exited warehouses and closed some manufacturing operations prelaunch, but this was low-hanging fruit few could argue about.

While this was going on, we had to keep the businesses running and people focused, all the while negotiating with 3M. This involved patents, real estate, logistics, plants, and so forth, worldwide as well as in the U.S. At the same time we had to organize and develop a new company, create systems, structure and reporting, as well as put leadership in place all over the world. There was a lot on our plate.

How the Name Came to Be

We hired a company, Interbrand, to help us create a name that reflected what we wanted to be. Everyone in the company could volunteer ideas for names. Interbrand came up with a list of computer-generated monikers. All of it was put together, sifted through and considered. In the end, it came down to two or three names and logos.

Viable names not already taken or registered were difficult to come by and "Imation" was the winner. Interbrand came up with the brand from the fact our business would succeed based on Imagination and Innovation and would exist in the Information and Imaging industries. The Imation name could be tied to all four.

Was the name successful? I'll have to say yes, but it's because our people made it successful. It wasn't easy. By itself, Imation didn't really mean anything. People call it EYE-mation, the same folks who call Italians EYE-talians. This used to bother me, but finally I decided, call us whatever you want. Just call us.

Getting the branding right was a challenge. We tried to be avant-garde with all the latest colors, and a lot of different ones were used in the seven businesses. One of them I lovingly referred to as "pond scum green." About three years into the process, we decided to make more changes. Red and black were the two colors that were going to have the most chance of breaking through and being remembered, so we picked red as our primary corporate color. We modified the logo to be larger and to fit into a block, taking the fancy one Interbrand had developed and reworking it so we ended up with twice as much impact in the same amount of space. If you look at a catalog that displays our brand along with competitors' like Fuji and Maxell, you'll see a big difference compared to the old days. We jump right off the page.

We had an unusual experience when we launched our Imation name and logo. The logo was a hand holding a magic wand which was spreading digital data (0s and +s) around above it. It was a striking and memorable graphic design. Immediately, however, we got feedback anonymously from employees saying the hand resembled a sign from the devil. It was very hard to believe people would actually construe this, but apparently some did. This was not a make or break issue, but we did change the hand a bit to eliminate any possible misperception or potential distractions. As a turnaround, avoiding distractions was important, and keeping people focused on critical business was imperative and worth a little trouble.

Looking back with 20-20 hindsight, what I learned was you're better off if you can find a real word to use when you name your company. Of course, whatever it is needs to translate well into other languages. But a real name is easier to remember than a computer generated one. For example, "Mosaic" is a new company that's a spinoff from Cargill—a real name, a memorable one, that apparently hadn't already been snapped up. This will be an advantage as they develop their reputation.

A Lot of Work to Do

Branding was only a small part of what had to be done in the seven months between the announcement and the official spinoff. We had to finish all the public filing documents, which entailed thousands and thousands of reports and more than twenty contracts with 3M. In addition, we had to:

- Create a management team
- Review assets and determine what we could afford (We wrote off and left with 3M a brand new but inefficient coater in Japan)
- Review all sites, plants and labs
- Create a benefit program
- Create new reporting systems
- Install an information management system worldwide (an ERP system). This actually was done over 18 months, while we leased space on 3M's system
- Establish new supply chain system going from more than 50 warehouses to slightly more than ten. (In Europe, from 28 to one.)
- Hold onto customers and build credibility.
- Make money

Customers were a big concern because without them, there would be no company to spin off. Let's face it, in a situation such as this, they're bound to be concerned about whether you're going to make it. They have to be asking themselves, "Should I stick with you when doing so could put my business at risk?" Our competitors jumped on this uncertain situation and worked to instill concerns and fear into our customers about the new company. That's why we spent a lot of time with them face to face and communicating with them by phone and email.

We also had to build a new office building and laboratory. All of our people were cohabiting with 3M and we had to move them out. We got the Oakdale office park in the spin. 3M gave us two buildings and 150 acres. It was good of them to let us have this because they didn't have to. It underscored the advantage of spinning off from a culture like 3M. First, we built a building to get the marketing people over from 3M. Then, it took a couple of years to finance and build a 450,000 square foot laboratory for R&D.

As those of you who have been through a spinoff have experienced, it is a complex and arduous task to plan and carry off, successfully. In any major change like this, both the parent and the new company will rely on dedicated and skilled employees to make it happen. At Imation, we could not have met SEC requirements, documentation needs and completed everything on time for the spinoff date without the outstanding effort and work of key people like Jill Burchill, Cathy Sams, and Brad Allen. And 3M could not have pulled off their part of what needed to be done without great legal and financial work led by Gregg Larson and Ron Nelson, among others.

We also relied on engineers like Barry Melchoir, and marketers led by Dennis Farmer, all of whom demonstrated the courage and dedication to make it happen.

3M Wants to Hold onto Value

Even though the top executives of 3M wanted us to succeed, they quite naturally were interested in holding onto value and wanted as little as possible of the company's intellectual property (IP) to get outside the business. They also wanted to protect their brands. A lot of people at

3M now saw the new company as a threat, even if it did add value for their shareholders. So, you might say there was a certain level of conflict. 3M didn't want bad press. They didn't want problems hanging on, but at the same time, they wanted to make sure Imation didn't get anything they didn't want us to have. At times negotiations became very tense. And there were lots of negotiations. Each one of the contracts had to be hammered out. Believe me, there was a good deal of circling of the wagons. The only leverage I had was to refuse to sign contracts and thereby threaten to delay the timing of the spin. That's not something you can credibly get away with at every turn. You have to be careful when and where you use it, but as you'll see, I did pull it out of my hat when I absolutely felt I had to. And it worked.

One piece of advice I have is to find people at the parent company who really, deep down, want to see you win. They are the ones who helped us through a grueling seven-month process. All the necessary filings with the SEC had to be made. All the agreements and decisions had to be completed on what's going, and what's staying with the mother ship. Often, I was surprised at who supported me and who didn't. The CEO had to be careful not to appear to take sides with the part of the company that was leaving. His role was to protect 3M's interests. So he stayed fairly aloof and objective. But there were 3M people who were key to getting it all done. People like Chuck Kiester, Dick Lidstad, Bill Coyne, Harold Wiens, and Gregg Larson helped Imation get started right.

Negotiating Intellectual Property Rights

Over that first half-year we had to negotiate all IP rights, and 3M was holding on tight to them. We had to have them in order to be a viable company and we were not getting very far. One day I called Marvin Mann, who was CEO of Lexmark and had managed the split of that company from IBM. His advice was that IP was so critical I needed to give it number one priority and attend every meeting between the companies on it.

"They cannot be allowed to meet unless you're in the room," he said. "These are the core decisions for your company's future."

So that's what I did. I was involved in every single negotiating session on IP. Eventually we were able to construct an IP arrangement that was satisfactory. It protected our rights and 3M's rights and prevented the possibility of 3M's technology being used against them in the future. It became our highest priority and the successful outcome allowed us to be a viable entity in our markets.

Negotiations Get Tense

We also had to negotiate a supply agreement on all products for which 3M supplied materials such as chemicals or film. Naturally, we didn't want to be held hostage by the terms of an unfavorable contract. These negotiations almost derailed the spin. Few people know it, but I refused to sign the supply agreement the day before the spin was to become official, the day the final documents were to be signed. I was in a room with Gregg Larson, 3M's lawyer. The 3M board meeting to complete the separation of Imation was going to be held the following day. I signed one document after the other, knowing I wasn't going to sign the supply agreement. I'd planned this ahead of time because I felt it was the only way we were going to get what was necessary to succeed. I had no other leverage but to dig in my heels with all the 3M board members already jetting their way into town. What the executives of the 3M division in charge of supply were sticking to put us at risk, and could literally put us out of business at some point. I simply couldn't let that happen.

I came to the supply agreement and set it aside. then I continued with the rest of the documents.

Gregg said, "Bill, you missed a document."

I said, "No, I didn't. I'm not signing that one."

He said, "What do you mean, you're not signing it?"

"I'm not signing that document. I've said all along, I'm not taking 12,000 people out of this company and putting them at risk with a supply agreement that puts our destiny in someone else's hands. I won't do it."

"What are we going to do?" Greg said.

I said, "Better get the people in the room who can change it."

So he called the lawyers who'd negotiated this supply agreement, who worked for the business unit that owned the supply.

The lawyer came into the room with a couple of her minions by her side, looked me in the eye and said,

"What's your problem?"

I replied, "I don't have any problems. As far as I can see, *you* have a problem. You'd better decide if you want the spin to go forward because I'm not signing that agreement."

"You know I don't have the authority to change it," she said.

"Then you'd better go back to your boss and figure it out," I replied.

She left in a huff.

Gregg and I sat in the room for about two and a half hours staring at each other, wondering what would come next—the very definition of tension.

Then she came back and asked, "What will you sign?"

From there we negotiated an agreement that was fair and that has worked for many years. This brought home that very often getting the right executive involved personally, not just the negotiators, is crucial to striking a fair deal.

Know the Other Fellow's Interest

There's another lesson to be learned from this that we've put to work in negotiations many times since then. The day before the board was to meet, 3M's driving interest was to get the deal done. No one at the supply division wanted to be responsible for having stopped the spin. My interest—Imation's interest—was to negotiate a supply agreement we could live with. Without a ticking clock, I had no leverage to do this.

The lesson is this. Know your key interest, know the other side's key interest, and negotiate for a win-win. We got a viable supply agreement and it didn't stand in the way of the deal.

Imation now uses a formalized process called Alignor® to put this interest-based negotiation process to work. Alignor will be discussed in more detail in Chapter Ten.

Use of the 3M Brand

In 1996, almost no one had yet heard of Imation, and it was clear we would need the use of the 3M name for some period of time until the Imation brand could be established. 3M is a respected company and a well-known brand name. Fortunately, we were able to negotiate rights for the use of the brand for three to five years.

Our agreements called for a phase out over a period of time, so that 3M's branding would be displayed in decreasing amounts until finally it wasn't used at all. During that period of time we were shipping huge numbers of floppy disks, which gave the 3M name visibility in offices all across the globe. This exposure clearly had value to 3M, which made the negotiation of a good deal easier than it might otherwise have been. Nevertheless, we took the position we wanted to get away from the 3M brand as quickly as possible and establish our own long term identity. For example, Matchprint® was a well-known brand among printers and graphic artists, so it became Imation Matchprint immediately.

The 3M name on diskette packages remained the longest. In exchange for the exposure this provided 3M, they gave us the use of the brand on other products on a royalty-free basis. "IMATION: Born of 3M innovation" was our transitional line. We followed a step-by-step plan so that 3M was off most of the products at the end of two years. All our products bore the Imation brand at the end of the third year.

Make the Break as Quickly as Possible

An important thing we learned, which may be of benefit to you, is that it's best to separate from the mother ship as quickly as possible. Until there's a physical break, it is virtually impossible to create a new corporate culture. This became strikingly apparent. In countries where we separated completely and did not cohabit with 3M, we became a separate, independent, aggressive and self-sufficient entity much faster than in places where we shared space.

This came home to me when I was visiting a plant just before Christmas 1996 where 3M was renting twenty-five percent of the space from us—so both companies were under one roof. At a meeting of the shop-floor workers, one of them said, "We don't think it's fair. 3M gave everyone a turkey for Christmas. All the 3M employees got a turkey, and we didn't."

The company was still very new and to get people charged up, we'd given everyone in the company stock options. Production line workers had received one hundred shares.

"Excuse me," I said. "You received 100 stock options. Today those 100 options are worth $700. That's a lot of turkey."

Well, I learned two things. First, we'd be better off to get completely away from 3M as quickly as possible. Second, to some employees, stock options were of little or no value—merely questionable pieces of paper.

In Italy, 3M spun off nearly half of its total business in that country, which included Medical Imaging and Photo Film. Faced with a lot of empty space, 3M gave us a great deal on co-habitation. We tried to find other space but weren't able to locate any that suited us well, so we took 3M's offer. This could be one of the worst decisions we made. Our Italian employees just weren't able mentally to make the break. After the two-year contract was up, 3M offered an even better deal for us to stay, but we moved on because by then we had realized things just weren't going to improve as long as we were under the same roof. It was what we had to do to establish a completely independent Imation.

LESSONS LEARNED:

- A huge amount of work is involved in a tax-free spin off and your key legal and financial people are vital to pull it off.
- If at all possible, find a name that already means something when you name your new company.
- Don't try to be cute with branding unless you're in a field that calls for cute. Stick to bright and bold.
- Put a high priority on Intellectual Property rights negotiations.
- Know the other party's interests and use these in your negotiations.
- Have a transition plan to move from the former parent company's brand to the new one. Treat this with urgency.
- Get away physically from the mother company as fast as possible so a new culture can take hold.
- Pick the people you know at the parent company who will step up, and rely on them to help you.
- Keep focus on your customers. Your competitors will attack during this uncertain time.

Chapter Three: People, the Most Important Asset

A company has brand names, reputation and notoriety, but a company is really only one thing—the sum of all its people and their work, good or bad. At spinoff, people were frightened and uncertain, concerned about their livelihood and bitterly disappointed at being "thrown out" of 3M. But Imation survived because the people it was comprised of were committed.

The employees are the heroes of Imation's story of survival and ultimate success. The leaders had to put people in the right places, motivate and direct them, but the courage and commitment of many of Imation's people in every country and in every department and function are what, in the long run, made success possible.

On July 1, 1996, our first official day, we held events to launch the company at all of our locations worldwide. These were high profile, high energy affairs because we viewed them as central to the effort of building confidence and spirit among employees, customers, shareholders and the local communities in which our facilities were located. Everything was coordinated and managed by our marketing and communications teams, led by Dennis Farmer and Will Sullivan. The inaugural events took place on the same day at every site in every country.

3M had been a family-oriented business, so we made these launches family affairs by inviting all employees and their families. We knew people felt uncertain. The goal was to show everyone—customers, suppliers, employees' families—we were real and were here to stay. We invited local politicians and customers. Our suppliers came. Governor Arnie Carlson of Minnesota attended the launch at our headquarters in Oakdale as well as Mayor Norm Coleman of St. Paul, who is now a U. S. Senator from Minnesota. It was important to illustrate our support of our communities and that we would be a solid corporate citizen.

Wherever possible we had these launches on company premises because we wanted them to be Imation events, and felt it was important for people to actually see the company and get a feel for it. At Oakdale, we set tents up on the property. One huge tent could accommodate the entire crowd. I gave the keynote address, and the Mayor of Oakdale spoke, as well as the Governor of Minnesota.

As an international company, we wanted these launches to be international events, so we had food from all over the world. In some countries, the U.S. ambassador was in attendance. And of course there were almost always local officials invited as was the case at headquarters in Oakdale. Making our launch a huge event helped us get off on the right foot and build needed momentum. We were taken seriously from day one in the local communities.

Optimism is Essential

Imation came into the world with $2.4 billion in sales and all the birth pains of a start-up. We had to launch in full flight and struggle from the beginning to keep a huge new company afloat while change was instituted. You might compare what we knew had to be done—launching a start up while managing structure and revenue totaling $2 billion—to climbing on a bucking bronco to tame it versus raising a colt from birth. Customers were nervous. Employees were nervous. And the shareholder base needed to be turned over since 3M shareholders who received the Imation stock in the spinoff were not natural candidates to hold a turnaround company like Imation.

Putting forth a vision for success is critical, but let's be realistic. Demonstrating optimism isn't always easy. When a bad quarter comes along, and things are coming down all around you, and new products aren't coming on fast enough, it's tough to leave the office with a smile on your face. But I quickly learned, you'd darn well better or you create so much uncertainty it can be very harmful. People are always watching. This is especially true in a tight, uncertain business that's struggling to get off the ground. If the top executives project a positive attitude, it carries over. If you take on an attitude of gloom and doom, that attitude will set a negative tone. This is a huge factor in turnarounds and start ups. The attitude of the leaders creates the attitude of the employees. This leads to an inevitable conclusion. Sometimes leaders must be moved out because they are unable to exude a positive attitude. Only an optimistic attitude can create a winning atmosphere.

It's impossible to place too much emphasis on this. Optimism and a positive attitude are critical to a successful turnaround. The situation may look dire, the mountain may look insurmountable, you may be weary, but there is no option. In order to survive, you must reach the goals you've set. You, the leader, must believe you can do it, and you must exude that confidence and build optimism in others so that the entire management team believes. A host of books have been written on this subject including *The Power of Positive Thinking, The Power of Thinking Big,* and *The Power of Believing.* In *Think and Grow Rich,* author Napoleon Hill says a management team with a common purpose and a positive attitude can be compared to a number of storage batteries hooked up in a series, instead of each one standing alone. The output is greatly magnified because they are linked. What you can't afford is a dead cell siphoning off power, or shorting out the group because its positive and negative leads are turned in an opposite direction.

Find Positive Leaders

It's human nature to become pessimistic in a difficult situation. An individual may say, "We can't possibly do this. It's too hard. The glass is half empty, not half full." You can't allow this kind of talk, or thinking. If a person doesn't believe, he doesn't belong in a leadership position. How many great football coaches do you suppose say "Things don't look good, boys," before the big game? A leader must generate the excitement to take on the challenge and the enthusiasm to make things work. If you are old enough, you may recall the Reagan years, and his "Shining City on the Hill," and be able to contrast that with the gloom and doom years of Jimmy Carter. Not many of us would like to live through those again. Optimism is made, not born.

People want to rally around a challenge such as the one John F. Kennedy gave in a famous address, which was to reach the moon before the end of the 1960s. Just as they were then, people are ready to take on an enormous challenge, but they must have positive leadership and see optimism and purpose in the eyes of the leaders.

A CEO must find and develop people who share a "can do" attitude if the team is to win. The CEO must keep the dream destination, the goal to be reached, out in front of the group where it is in view at all times. He or she must focus the organization on success and knock off whatever obstacles are in the way one at a time, creating change to overcome any setbacks along the way. The CEO must set goals that at times look unattainable but stretch the organization to do better. The CEO must be relentless.

Thomas Troward, a metaphysician who lived about a hundred years ago, believed as Carl Jung did that all of us are connected though our subconscious minds. He thought this resulted in what might be called a group mind. He believed this group mind is programmed by our conscious minds to arrange things, such as the people one meets and the events that take place, so that the reality we think about and expect is the reality we get. I don't know if Troward was correct, but my experience has been that leaders who think big, have a positive outlook and high expectations, are much more likely to get positive results than those who dwell on all the things that might go wrong. Of this, there can be no question.

You, as a leader, must search out the positive people on your team, the optimists, and support that optimism and their courage in facing difficult situations. Pessimists can sometimes be helpful in identifying potential problems optimists may overlook, but they can't be put in positions where they are leading others. Leadership must be positive about the ability to change, improve, and eventually to win.

Expect the Stages of Change

Many Imation employees who came from 3M felt they'd been betrayed. Dr. Elisabeth Kübler-Ross, author of the famous book *On Death and Dying*, identified five stages everyone goes through when they face life-altering change. Many former 3Mers got stuck in one or another of the stages, so be on the lookout if your company goes through a spinoff or major turnaround that pulls the rug out from under people.

Stage One is denial, as in, "There's been a mistake. I'm sure 3M had guaranteed me lifetime employment. This can't be happening." Yet the person's name is right there on Newco's organization chart. This reaction is normal. The person is stunned. It will take a while for reality to sink in.

"This isn't happening," he or she may say. "If I just keep my head down and smile, all this will blow over." Of course, it does not blow over, and eventually the person realizes the change is real.

Next, is anger.

"I can't believe they did this to me—after all my hard work and what I've accomplished. They have no appreciation for what I've done. They will be sorry."

If you're lucky, people will get past the anger and move on to the next stage, which is bargaining.

"Okay, I understand, now. Like it our not, I'm part of this new company. But can't we structure it like the old company? Can't we have the same benefits? We had great medical and retirement plans. I'll be happy and do my job if this new company will just guarantee me a cushy job with lifetime employment and great benefits the same as the old company did."

The people who came to Imation found bargaining did no good, and some progressed to the fourth stage, which is depression. A change in body language could be seen. Slumped shoulders. Dark circles under the eyes, it's as though the individual was saying, "Goodness knows, I've tried. I simply don't deserve this." Then the complaining and finger pointing started taking up time and attention.

It may not seem so, but once a person has reached this stage, there is hope. If he or she is not too far along on the career path, or is not too set in his or her ways, the individual will move on to the fifth and last stage, which is acceptance. Then you're home free. You've got yourself a team player. Unfortunately, many Imation employees were too attached to 3M. They got stuck in stage four and became a negative factor in the company.

Consider Coaching Those in Stage Four

It may be helpful to coach them. It is worth a try to explain that what they're going through is normal and there are techniques one can use to speed up passage through the various stages to acceptance. You could, for example, hand them a copy of this book with this section marked.

Here's something for them to think about. In his book, *The Seven Habits of Highly Effective People,* Stephen Covey writes about a realization that altered his life. He was wandering among stacks of books in a college library when he came across one that drew his interest. He opened it and was so moved by what he read that he reread the paragraph many times. It contained the simple idea that a gap exists between stimulus and response, and that the key to our growth and happiness is how we use this gap. We have the power to choose in that fraction of a second.

Abraham Lincoln is reported to have said most people are about as happy as they decide to be. Think about it. If we walk by a Dairy Queen and see a photograph of a frothy chocolate milk shake, we can choose to order and eat it, or we can decide to skip dessert. We don't have to be slaves to our knee jerk reactions.

Richard Carlson, the author of *Don't Sweat the Small Stuff . . . and It's All Small Stuff,* picks up on the same idea. His advice is always to take a breath before speaking or taking action. People who adopt this can rid themselves of the habit of reacting. Instead, they can begin taking a considered approach. Taking a considered approach can lead to all sorts of good things such as a positive attitude at work.

Another way is to become what some have called a "silent observer" of yourself. The idea is to move your point of view out of your head, and place it on your shoulder or on the ceiling. Then watch yourself go about your business. Once you start keeping an eye out, you may see things you're doing that aren't helping you get where you want to go. From there, it's a short step to move on to acceptance and a positive attitude. Especially if you take that breath before reacting.

Training and Coaching to Get People Past the Hump

The ideas just covered, especially accompanied by training and coaching, can help people deal with realities and build optimism. When we were in our darkest days at Imation, our team developed a program we called, "The Wave of Change." This was a series of off-site meetings of forty to fifty key employees at a time. They came from all levels, all functions, and all countries. Each "Wave" session was made up of a diverse group of people with one common denominator—they were critical to our success. Our top executives put on the session, sharing our vision and our plans, why we were doing what we were doing and how we expected to succeed. We communicated our corporate vision and direction, each business unit's plan, financial plan, and our human resources and legal process and plan. We emphasized International and our worldwide opportunities.

One very important part of our agenda was "The Customer Perspective." We invited our customers and they came and led these sessions for us. We held group brainstorming on how Imation would become more customer focused and what each of us could do to be more accountable for Imation's results and what we could personally do to affect change and create urgency.

These getaways started as two-day sessions but we refined them over time into one-day sessions plus a team dinner. We held one a quarter and maintained a very open environment with lots of hands on by our executives. This initiative helped us hold the company together during a very critical and difficult time.

As we progressed, we added to our training programs. We offered functional training to the entire company, and we started mentoring and coaching programs which are still in place today. In 2002-3 we established a "Leadership Development Program" that is one week long and uses outside trainers as well as inside executives. It is great for team building and focuses on Financial Discipline, Interest-Based Negotiation, Ethics and Honesty, Process Driven Excellence, and Leadership. These sessions are held three times a year for employees worldwide. Mini sessions, one to two days, are also provided for large numbers of employees in the U.S. and other major countries.

Training is crucial to improvement. Our experience has been that everyone wants to succeed, but people need the tools to do so, which makes training and coaching key success factors.

Leave the Wounded

Some former 3Mers got too wrapped up in their own pain to move very far along the five stages of adjustment to change. Some never got past anger. Others moved along a short way and then got mired in depression. They just could not seem to get though those four stages to acceptance. It's understandable, perhaps. Being spun off from 3M had a real impact on their lives. It happened unexpectedly. They felt betrayed—left behind. But whether they realized it or not, they did have a choice. They could choose to look at being part of a new company as an exciting opportunity, or they could see it as a disaster.

Some very smart people failed because they could not resist looking back and longing for the old life. They lacked the optimism and spirit to carry a tough challenge forward. Some very talented people did not stay the course because this was not what they had signed up for at 3M. They disliked the massive change that had to be implemented and the very difficult, non-3M-like decisions that had to be made. These people created a serious problem. It wasn't long before we came to the realization we had to leave the wounded in order to survive. This may sound cold, but all our energy was required for survival. A new company's focus, or that of a turnaround, must be on the people who will make change happen, and who have the enthusiasm and commitment to succeed. We had to get management to understand this, which was difficult for many, especially those who had been at 3M for up to thirty years. So, the people who were not willing or able to be part of the change simply had to go. We dealt with them as humanely as possible, we provided outplacement services, but did not look back. Speed was critical, and these people put others' jobs at risk.

People are a company's most vital asset, but you can

have too many people, and you can have the wrong people. Those who are committed deserve leadership that is willing to step forward and make the changes necessary to insure everyone is productive and contributing.

Don't Talk Anyone into a Job

Regardless of someone's ability, a person has to have the right attitude if they are going to succeed and be a valuable contributor. This leads to a bit of advice about something I learned the hard way. Don't talk anyone into staying. In any situation like this, whether it's a merger or a spinoff, some people are going to be on the fence. Take it from me, if they don't want to stay, you can't afford to keep them because they are likely to become the dead battery that short circuits the whole group.

One man I wanted badly to come with us was a brilliant young coater engineer. He was in the unusual position of having a choice. Though he was employed in one of the spinoff business units, 3M recognized his considerable abilities and was willing and able to find a place for him so he could stay. This guy was really good. I tried to talk him into coming with the new company.

I said, "You know, we will be investing a lot of money in coating. You'll probably be right in the thick of the most advanced coating developments in the world."

"Gee, I don't know," he said.

"Think about it," I said. "It's not like you have to relocate. You'll be living in the same town where you grew up. Coating is what you've been studying all your life. You're going to be working on the most sophisticated technology in the world if you come with us—using some of the most advanced coaters the world."

"Yeah," he said. "But when I sit down with my family for Thanksgiving dinner, I'm the only one there who doesn't work for 3M, and I want that to change."

Obviously, he came from a 3M family, which wasn't all that unusual in Minnesota. Still, his attitude made no sense to me. But how could I argue with it? He wanted to be with 3M no matter how good the opportunities were elsewhere. You're better off not to waste time convincing someone like that to stay because there will be regrets on both sides if he does.

Attitude is Everything

A great many people who came from 3M shook off their depression quickly. 3M company provided most of our productive leaders. One such key leader was our VP of International, Dave Wenck. This guy has international business in his blood. Dave wasn't afraid of the challenge or of change. He thrived on it. He's a stocky, straight-forward leader with a strong financial background, and business experience all over the world. He was Managing Director of 3M Singapore, and Business Comptroller of 3M Europe, as well as Regional Comptroller for Latin America and Asia, and General Manager of the Optical and CD ROM businesses. I would describe him as very conservative, principled and stubborn. He is also committed, loyal and aggressive. People get clear direction from Dave and like working for him. He was a helicopter pilot in Vietnam and took into business the toughness he gained from that experience. People who like Dave refer to him as "Captain Wenck." His "can-do" attitude carried over to our international employees and definitely helped us succeed.

Dave was one of the executives who set the tone for the company, but many others stepped up as well and took on the challenge, even though it was not what they had bargained for at 3M.

This was also true of many employees in the spin who were on lower rungs of the corporate ladder at that time. For example, the current CFO of Imation, Paul Zeller, came as an accountant for one of the business units in the spin.

We were also fortunate to convince a lot of women to come over, perhaps because they perceived a glass ceiling to exist at 3M. Many believed we offered a unique opportunity. And you know what? They were right. Imation gave them an opportunity to put their talent to work, to advance faster, and they took it. They stepped up to the challenges and made things happen. Often, they were the ones who led the way through tough times, embracing change, dealing with disappointment, and setting positive examples for the rest of us. Their optimistic outlooks were contagious and became the glue that held people together through many battles.

Volunteers Lead the Way

Success at Imation was built by the employees who came over from 3M, put the past behind them, and saw opportunity in the challenges facing our new company. Many stepped up, carried the heavy loads, and stayed the course even when our future looked grim.

Another group I call "3M volunteers" had an enormous impact on our long term success. I call them volunteers because they came from 3M voluntarily. They left solid positions in places all over the world and joined us even though they understood the challenges and business issues we faced. Perhaps, since they made a conscious choice to join us, they didn't have to pass through the mental stages of change, or face the regrets others did who were cast adrift. They faced the tough times with resolve and remained positive and optimistic. Many of these volunteers, recruited by Dave Wenck, Dennis Farmer, and myself, became long term leaders for the company. They shared our vision for success, not just for survival.

Some of these include Nobuyoshi Kawasaki who started our Japan operations and now leads all of Asia, and Raymond Yeung, who heads the China region. Jackie Chase left a position in the 3M legal department and has become Vice President Human Resources. She has played a critical role in all our restructuring and training and development initiatives. Frank Russomano left 3M as a marketing director and rose to COO of Imation. Ron Hansen, another volunteer from 3M, has developed a very strong Latin American business. Larry Eaton, an Executive Vice President at 3M, volunteered to be on our Board and provided invaluable guidance and support to me personally throughout our formative years.

Look Inside First for Your Leaders

After the spinoff, people exhibited very different reactions to this crisis in their lives. There were those who could not cut the umbilical cord and focused entirely on getting back to 3M. And there were people who looked forward to building a new successful company, who had a "we'll show you" attitude toward our former parent. For example, the volunteers talked about who came by choice to fill key slots viewed this new company as the challenge and opportunity of a lifetime—one to be embraced.

I've found that in a difficult business, leaders will emerge from inside the organization more often than from the outside. While we found that not every leader appointed by 3M could take us to the next level, longer-term leaders emerged from the lower levels of Imation by bringing attention to themselves as a result of their achievements. These men and women demonstrated the personal commitment necessary to lead. An example is Imation's present COO, Frank Russomano, who volunteered to come from 3M to Imation on a lateral move at the director level. He's an aggressive, east-coast guy, who is smart, tough and committed. Frank is a real competitor in tough business fights and a good negotiator. He took on the many difficult challenges thrown his way, such as corporate marketing, where he helped to greatly reduce the cost structure. He also stepped up to the challenge of a struggling Superdisk program, unraveled the company from a highly expensive R&D initiative, and took on the challenge of focusing and improving our Data Storage Tape business. Frank demonstrated the value of personal commitment to the team and to his job. Fortunately, there were many others like Frank at Imation. They exist at every company. The trick is to recognize who they are and give them opportunities to demonstrate what they can do.

At Imation, I'd say we had less than a fifty percent success rate when it came to outside hiring. When you hire from the outside, you know the upside but you never know the downside. With insiders, you usually will have a good appreciation of both their strengths and weaknesses. Because of this, you are in a better position to determine how to use their talents in the most productive way. Also, you will have a pretty good idea up front if a real personal commitment exists. When you go outside to hire someone, you have to hope the commitment will be there.

My advice is to bet on people inside the company who have experience in your industry. My experience indicates having a knowledge of the industry and products and business forces at work greatly improves an executive's chances for success. As I look back over the many years I was at 3M, the divisions in the company that performed well most often were those that enjoyed a continuity of leadership—leaders who possessed in-depth knowledge of the customers and products of the division they ran. These were not the anointed ones who were put in jobs to gain experience on their way up the corporate ladder, but the people who performed and delivered at each level, learning along the way.

There can be no doubt. People who lacked the talent,

experience, or work ethic necessary to operate at an acceptable level in these businesses were exposed by the challenging environment they found themselves in, while at the same time those who would create the new company emerged. It became apparent during the first few years at Imation that experience and success were linked. People who knew the businesses, possessed the inner drive and had acquired the requisite skills were the ones who led the way and saved the company. Outside hiring played an important role and generated needed initiative and energy at key times, but the experienced people in our businesses were the ones who did the heavy lifting, stayed the course and carried Imation to success. They were the ones who knew what it would take to win, and perhaps more important than anything, they were the ones who most wanted to win.

Key people in every area of Imation stepped forward and used their experience to make success happen. They were not deterred by setbacks and bad quarters. As long as they knew the direction we were headed and why, they kept pushing forward.

Key Positions Filled from the Inside

Key executive positions filled from the inside include our previously-mentioned Vice President of Human Resources, Jackie Chase, and our Manufacturing and Supply Chain Vice President, Colleen Willhite. Colleen had the knowledge of our products and operations and is very skilled in the areas of cost reduction and quality improvement. She has played a vital role in our operations throughout our history.

Paul Zeller contributed at every level of Finance, dating from our spinoff. He became our comptroller in 1998 and CFO in 2004. The comptroller's role in restructuring, cost cutting, acquisitions, and now Sarbanes Oxley, is one of the most important in any company.

Imation, through trial and error, acting and changing, evolved a very strong and diverse management team.

Outside Hires Make a Difference Too

As mentioned above, we also found our turnaround needed specific skills and experience we did not possess in house. 3M was a large, successful multinational corporation with strong support staffs and backup at every level. Imation was a smaller turnaround that had to be lean. We simply did not have all the skills we needed in place. We had to go outside to find these.

We made mistakes when we hired from the outside to be sure, but we also were successful hiring people who played key roles in driving long term success. In 1998, for example, we brought in a CFO, Robert Edwards, who played a critical part in our restructuring and was a most aggressive and successful champion in our drive for cash and financial discipline. We hired John Sullivan as our General Counsel in 1998. John has played vital roles in our successful divestitures, provided excellent guidance and leadership to us on all our legal matters, and set a strong governance attitude for our company that was an important complement to the ethics and honesty training and culture we brought with us from 3M.

Brad Allen, our Vice President of Investor Relations and later Vice President of Corporate Communications, was another outside hire who made a big contribution. His Wall Street contacts and his experience were incredibly valuable as we developed and changed as a company. He kept our investors in the boat all along the way.

Diversity Prevents Myopia

This leads to another important point, which is the value of a diverse workforce. By diverse, I do not mean only race, gender, age or sexual orientation. When it comes to moving a business forward, diversity of thought is as important as other differences. This includes extroverts and introverts, R&D's viewpoint, as well as sales and marketing flash and glitter. You must avoid one style only emerging in leadership, or you can end up with a biased team where everyone thinks the same way and alternative but effective approaches are missed. Respecting peoples' differences leads to positive interaction, as well as the ability to listen to and consider creative options.

As stated earlier, you certainly want leaders who are optimistic and have positive attitudes. But this doesn't mean you ought to chose only those who think the same way you do. According to the Myers-Briggs system for categorizing personalities, there are sixteen basic types. Imagine how myopic the leadership of a company would be if all its leaders had the same one. Yet this can happen if you are not careful. It seems as though, when it comes to selecting the right person for a job, we often talk out of both sides of our mouths. While we say that "variety is the spice of life" when putting together a staff, what we actually do tends to look a whole lot more like cloning. The reason is understandable. At work and at play, things seem to go more smoothly when we're with people who are very much like ourselves.

The fact is, whether hiring is done in individual departments or by a centralized personnel department, most staffs invariably resemble those at the top in terms of personality type. More often than not, these top executives share preferences for objective decision making as well as structure, precise scheduling, and order. It's not that those who don't share these traits are incompetent. It's just that in a system driven by profits and productivity, those who possess them have the edge. Other types, however qualified, are often destined to leave the organization prematurely.

This is not to say those who rely on intuition and make decisions based on how something makes them feel—as opposed to strict logic—cannot cut it in the management world. Many do. In fact, according to authorities on this subject, all sixteen types can be found in management positions of major corporations and government agencies. Still, the overwhelming majority fall into "Thinking and Judging" (TJ) category as opposed to "Intuitive-Feeling" (IF). Yet having people around who bring a different perspective to things is extremely beneficial to out-flanking your competition.

An office full of TJs will view the world in largely black-and-white terms. Things will be either right or wrong. When two TJs disagree, one sees black and the other sees white. In this case, there will be few alternative solutions short of pulling rank and status, shouting more loudly, or becoming increasingly more stubborn. Sometimes the source of the disagreement can become obscured—are the parties disagreeing with the matter at hand, or are they reacting to the fact that they can see themselves in each other? Often it's hard to tell. In the end, productivity becomes curtailed.

Contrast this to a working environment in which a broader mix of types is found. Studies show that diversity engenders creativity. The more diversity of personnel on any given task, the better the final product will be, if (a) differences are respected, authenticated, and integrated; and (b) communication remains open. Clearly, with so many opposing points of view, projects may take longer to accomplish, but the end result will have more people committed to it because more people had a chance to influence the process, and there will be a greater sense of pride. Also, a strong leader will have the opportunity to listen to all points of view, then to choose and move aggressively and quickly.

At one time or another most managers have been through the management training exercise in which they are lost at sea—or in a desert or on the moon—as the result of a crash. All that's left are a handful of specific items, ranging from a case of scotch to a small mirror to a piece of cheese. The task they're given is to rank-order the items in terms of their importance to survival.

In this exercise each manager must independently come up with his or her own rank order. Then groups of managers are assigned to arrive at some consensus of the ranking. This process parallels real-life group decision making—you arrive at the meeting with some opinions, a little knowledge, and your reactions to the people with whom you must work to reach a group decision.

The final scores in this training exercise are usually set against some "expert" criteria. Repeatedly, groups that have the widest diversity of knowledge, a group ranging for example from a former Marine who's an expert in desert survival to an accountant who's never spent a night under the stars, will come up with the list most closely aligned to the "correct" answers—provided the group respects their diversity and communicates openly about differences of opinion.

Along with such diversity comes a variety of perspectives to just about every situation. Not everyone will have the same view of punctuality. There will be differences in work styles. A single parent will have a different perspective on what constitutes "full-time work" than will a married person with grown kids. A sixty-year old employee will deal with a fast-paced travel schedule differently than a thirty-year-old. And so on. Nevertheless, diversity is good in that it will help your organization think outside the box, and thereby come up with creative solutions. The value is in what people can accomplish, not in how they do it.

LESSONS LEARNED:

- A high-profile launch can get things moving in the right direction.
- Optimism is essential. Thinking big and thinking positive will produce better results than dwelling on what might go wrong.
- A team that's positive and pushing toward the same goals will accomplish more than the same individuals working alone. Two and two does add up to five.
- A CEO must find leaders who are positive and weed out the negative.
- Don't talk anyone into taking a job they don't want.
- All leaders are not born. Tough challenges often cause them to emerge from the ranks. They are likely to have valuable firsthand experience in the business and have demonstrated commitment.
- You are likely to have more success and fewer headaches if you develop your future leaders from the inside. Go outside only for skills you don't have.
- People who face life-altering change will pass through four stages before they reach acceptance. Expect this and help coach people so they move along more quickly.
- All forms of diversity including that of thought, experience, style, background, and personality are very valuable. Better decisions result from bringing many perspectives and experiences to bear.

Chapter Four: Leadership, the Critical Element

As discussed in the previous chapter, there's no question people are a company's most valuable asset. No CEO, manager or supervisor, no matter how brilliant or talented, can do it all alone. Even the greatest leader will not go far without the support and efforts of a team that has what it takes to do the job. Success or failure will come as a result of the skills, attitudes, and actions of everyone down the line pulling together to move forward and get the job done. But even though dedication and the right skill sets are requisites for success, talented and capable employees aren't all that's needed to win. Something else is equally important. This something is what harnesses the available energy and talent and channels it toward a goal.

Whether it's a sports team, a school class, or a business, for the highest level of effectiveness to be reached, what's needed is solid and consistent leadership. Even a team comprised of outstanding individuals can falter unless a leader gets them working in harmony. Just consider some professional sports teams that have scads of talent but still don't make the playoffs.

Much has been written about leadership, some of it self-serving, some simplistic, some glorifying particular leaders. I believe great leadership can be boiled down to a single core attribute. This is *personal commitment* to the company, the team, or the objective everyone has bought into.

Personal commitment compels an individual to take the necessary actions and to have the courage to follow through and persevere until the goal is reached. Personal commitment aligns the thoughts and minds of the leader and the team so that the sum is greater than the parts and even unconscious actions lead toward positive results. And personal commitment breeds the most important ingredient of all, a bond of trust between team members and the leader, trust that the actions to be taken will lead to the best result. Think about it. People may respect another person's intellect but at the same time sense a person is not committed. Like it our not, most people simply are not going to follow someone they don't trust.

Mr. Bill George, former Chairman & CEO of Medtronic Inc., a very successful health care company in Minnesota, wrote about the attributes of a leader in his book, *Authentic Leadership.* He says leadership in a company is not the exclusive domain of the CEO, it needs to exist throughout the organization. He believes authentic leaders demonstrate five qualities:

- Understanding their purpose — Passion
- Practicing solid values — Behavior
- Leading with heart — Compassion
- Establishing connected relationships — Connected
- Demonstrating self-discipline — Consistency

These qualities cannot come about on their own and I believe will not be manifested unless the leader is personally committed to the endeavor and its success.

Many Types of Leaders

Successful leaders have demonstrated many different characteristics and styles over the years. Sometimes it seems the only thing they have in common is a burning commitment to success.

The Despot

Many examples can be cited of despots who were successful leaders—at least for a time. Examples include Stalin and Hitler. But not all who rule with an iron fist are emissaries of the dark side. Others, like former Green Bay Packers coach Vince Lombardi and World War II hero, General George Patton, were revered. Vince Lombardi summed up succinctly what was important to men like himself when he said, "Winning isn't everything, it's the only thing."

It's hard to argue these men weren't focused or committed.

The Quiet Introvert

Though quiet and reserved, this type of leader is typically successful due to extraordinary capabilities and fortitude, also coupled with an unshakable commitment to a goal. Those who come to mind include Dwight D. Eisenhower, Abraham Lincoln, Mahatma Gandhi, George Washington, New York Yankee's manager Joe Torre, former

UCLA basketball coach John Wooden, and perhaps the richest man in the world, Bill Gates. All might be described as soft-spoken. Nevertheless, they exude a sense of inner strength that appears as strong as steel. Their style of leadership can be glimpsed in a quote attributed to General Eisenhower, "Leadership is the art of getting someone else to do something you want done because he wants to do it."

The Star Leader

There is, of course, a third type of leader. This one has a certain star quality, something that might be described as charisma, which reflects a powerful personality and projects a larger than life persona. My list of those who measure up in this regard include Winston Churchill, Franklin Delano Roosevelt, John F. Kennedy, Alabama football coach Paul Bear Bryant, and former GE Chairman & CEO Jack Welsh.

THE POINT IS, many types of leaders exist, but it seems to me the trait they share is a high level of commitment to an endeavor, organization, or a goal. This is needed in order to have the courage and tenacity to continue ahead through the dark days. To those around them, such commitment is self evident and leads to the trust among followers written about above. The team comes to believe they can count on their leader to show the way. They are led by example. The leader will reinforce his team's trust by taking responsibility when misfortune occurs. And rather than take credit for achievements, great leaders build loyalty on top of trust by giving credit where credit is due—and perhaps sometimes even when it is not due. Consider how Ronald Reagan almost never took credit for the achievements of his administration, but instead was quick to praise his staff. In doing so he achieved a level of loyalty among his followers perhaps unprecedented in modern times.

What else is a great leader able to do? He or she is able to articulate a vision the team can easily grasp. As already mentioned, for Reagan it was his "Shining City on a Hill." The leader points the way for the team to proceed to the realization of the vision and in doing so generates optimism and bolsters belief the goal can be reached. And belief, as has been said, is powerful.

What else is there about great leaders?

Typically, they are good listeners. They want to know what others think, and do not believe they, themselves, always have the best or right answer. They are smart enough to use the intelligence and the experience of others, and understand a good idea can come from anywhere at any time. When a great leader comes in contact with an idea that makes good sense, he or she recognizes and heeds the sensation of truth that resonates within. In other words, the idea or thought just seems to "click." Timid or unsure individuals often will dismiss this feeling. Great leaders are secure with themselves. They see when someone else has a better idea and have the self-confidence to put that idea to work.

Great leaders also are demanding. They simply do not tolerate mediocrity. This may be one of the most difficult roles to play because it's human nature to want others to like you, and if you push people hard, they may not like it—or you. Nevertheless, great leaders review and evaluate, and demand improvement and excellence. Jack Welsh at General Electric was reported to be a master at this and had the reputation of constantly having driven his subordinates to the pinnacle of excellence. Vince Lombardi, Winston Churchill, and Louis Gerstner of IBM all used high expectations to achieve goals. They were willing to make the tough decisions and to bring them to reality.

Great leaders have and show respect for the people they lead, whether they be soldiers, employees, players, or citizens. They lead by example and in doing so demonstrate they are worthy of being followed. They are personally committed to the institution they head, as well as the objective of the institution, and are out front personally doing whatever they can to reach it. I know this from experience. The employees at Imation, for example, recognized right away which leaders were personally committed to the company and which were more interested in their own agendas.

A number of hires we made brought all this home to me. We went outside for some executives who came highly recommended by others in our industry. Needless to say, they had great contacts and used them. They were also very articulate, very intelligent, and by all appearances consummate executives. But, once on board, their people saw something else. The problem was, they viewed Imation as a stepping stone to bigger jobs down the road—a way station on a carefully mapped out route. People immediately picked up on this, and ascertained they were not truly valued by these leaders. In the end, the people they were assigned to lead refused to follow them. They knew, perhaps without fully articulating it, who was looking out for number one, and who was committed. This made the road a rough one—the team questioning the commitment of the leader.

It comes down to what the greatest leader of all time—judging by the number of followers he still has today—said 2000 years ago: "Whoever wants to be great among you must be your servant, and whoever wants to be first must be the slave of all." (Mt 20:26-27) In other words, you don't get to be and stay the leader by serving yourself and having others serve you. People follow because ultimately you are serving them. You do this as a result of your commitment and service to the whole.

IN SUMMARY, people at Imation quickly rallied around the true leaders, those who where committed to the company. The ego-centric executives had great difficulty developing true teams. My experience is that people are pretty much the same wherever they are, which means if you want to lead, you must dedicate yourself to your group and your cause. Listen to them, and put aside any thought of or inclination toward self-aggrandizement.

LESSONS LEARNED:

Successful leaders have been different in many ways but they have had many traits in common:

- Personal commitment to an institution, a cause, or an objective.
- Courage of conviction to stay the course during bad times as well as good.
- Optimism about eventual success that has the effect of motivating others in the organization.
- A clear, easy-to-understand vision and objectives that get everyone moving in the same direction toward the same goal.
- A willingness to explain when and why tough actions are necessary and the courage to take them.
- A willingness to push others to achieve excellence.
- A willingness to praise others and give credit where credit is due.
- A willingness to take responsibility for setbacks.
- The courage and ability to recognize a good idea and adopt it regardless of its source.

Chapter Five: Creating a Performance Culture

The survival of Imation was not a given at spin. The businesses we took over were not performing, and we no longer had 3M's deep pockets to bail us out if things didn't improve. It was clear we had to motivate people to achieve and to drive productivity with our policies. We needed to weed out those who were only along for the ride, biding their time to see if the company would survive. This is why we made a high-risk decision to dramatically change our culture from what it had been at 3M.

Change Started on Day One

We started to embrace change immediately and necessarily in November 1995, six months prior to the actual spinoff. I knew key decisions at that time would impact us for years, so we had to make sure we got off on the right foot. Things started with a bang.

Prior to my appointment as CEO, 3M had already made and announced major organizational decisions for the new company. This was done with good intentions. 3M management hoped to affect a smooth transition. But it was clear the new company needed to be different from 3M if it was to survive and prosper, and many of the decisions which had been made did not coincide with the need to change from the past in order to begin creating a culture that could win in Imation's tough business environments.

On my first weekend in the job, I realized I needed to undo right away some of what 3M had put in place. Within a week, I announced a change in the VP of Europe in order to get someone in that position I knew would be able to drive hard-nosed, needed change. The man I named to the job was Richard Northup, an extremely experienced international operator from the UK. Northup was a feisty Brit, experienced in difficult business situations in Europe and Australia. He was the sort of guy who took challenges head on and never backed away from hard decisions. A tough boss, he was an experienced leader, who had lived and worked in Australia, Italy and Paris as well as the UK. He had experience in tough turnarounds. His appointment wasn't popular among the ranks or with 3M executives, but it was one of my best decisions.

We also had to go against what 3M had already announced and change the plan for the European headquarters to be in Italy. It was clear that our headquarters needed to be in Holland where we would have a better tax rate and a more central location for our European leaders.

At the Top of the List, a New Culture

I had a definite idea in mind from day one of the culture I believed Imation needed. Above all else, it would be a culture that supported and promoted performance. We were fortunate to have been spun off by a company as solid and honorable as 3M. Perhaps the biggest benefit that company provided Imation was an outstanding legacy of honesty and integrity, and many examples of how to be the best possible corporate citizen and employer. This gave us a solid base on which to build—a platform for our culture—the hallmark of which was respect for others.

With this as our base, we set out these basic policies to help establish a new culture of performance:

- Non-communistic pay practices, i.e. salaries and raises based on the contribution made by an individual compared to peers
- Pay for performance, i.e. a percentage of an individual's compensation tied to reaching clearly defined goals
- No perks for anyone
- Employee ownership of the business through stock options
- The realization customers always come first
- A sense of urgency to get things done
- Timely and frequent recognition of a job well done
- Enhancement of employability through training to replace 3M's unwritten lifetime employment policy
- A cash balance pension instead of 3M's defined benefit plan, giving people the flexibility to stay or to leave if they did not want the challenge

Building Trust

Imation's chances for success lay in our people—our employees, customers, partners, suppliers and distributors all sticking with us as we turned our businesses around.

We needed to preserve the part of our 3M legacy that would bridge our first days as a new, unknown company into one with a solid future. We did not know all that the future would hold, or throw at us, but we knew that the values we put in place at the outset would be critical to our success. These values, which have remained unchanged since the first days of Imation, are:

- Delivering unsurpassed value to our customers, shareholders, employees and community
- Maintaining the highest level of integrity and honesty
- Valuing and respecting our people and their diversity
- Protecting the environment, the safety of our people and the respect of our local communities
- Providing the highest quality in everything we do

Building the trust of our employees, customers and shareholders was vital to our success. People support those they believe will act in an honest and ethical manner— those who have a strong set of values. You build a future though consistent adherence to your values regardless of the challenges that come along.

Our entire team worked very hard to establish our values and to live up to them. It allowed people to stay the course in tough times, knowing we could trust each other.

Many customers and shareholders will join in that trust when they are treated accordingly and consistently. Shareholders may become annoyed with our strict adherence to Regulation F.D., prohibiting any individual disclosures, but they respect this position. They trust companies that adhere to it and exhibit the correct values.

Say Good-bye to Complacency

Things changed overnight for those who were part of the spinoff. We were suddenly on our own without 3M to back us up, no huge cash supply to fall back on, and not a whole lot of time to make our own way in a rough and tumble world. Establishing a results-oriented company was critical to Imation's survival because of the highly-competitive industries we found ourselves in. The companies we were up against were mainly Japanese, including Fuji, Maxell, Sony, and Mitsubishi. Like many Japanese businesses, they used price cuts as the number one way to compete. We knew we could expect ten percent price erosion across our spectrum of products every year. We had to plan for this, drive costs lower to deal with it, and improve faster than our competition in order to win against this tactic.

To create a results-oriented culture, we had to overcome the natural human desire for security, lifetime employment, and the certainty that a comfortable pension would be waiting down the road. All these are extremely attractive, but unfortunately, in today's highly-competitive business world, they are no longer realistic expectations.

No More Lifetime Employment Guarantee

Many large corporations in the mid-nineties had huge

benefit packages, and an expectation existed that if you kept your nose clean, you would retire from the business. As we all know, now, in the twenty-first century, that world has changed. In Imation's case, lifetime employment was definitely unrealistic. We would surely be required to reduce costs every year and divest businesses. Even so, the development of people in an effort to bring out their potential was within our grasp. We decided it would be our policy to help people make themselves more valuable both to Imation and to other potential employers. So, along with other tactics we will discuss, we were able to create a major shift in culture by replacing the unwritten promise of lifetime employment people had felt at 3M with that of employability. We implemented this by providing opportunities for advancement, and by providing training. This made Imation an attractive place to work and helped us hold onto productive people. It is one reason Imation now has very experienced battle-hardened veterans around the world who set the tone and lead the company's success—people who came up through the ranks.

The policy paid off for Imation and for our people. One example is our new Chief Financial Officer, Paul Zeller, who at spin was an accountant for one of the business units. Before I left the company, he said, "Bill, I would have had maybe a few promotions in my career by now if I was still at 3M, but look where I am now because of the opportunity here."

Measure It, Achieve It

So there we were, in the deep end of the pool, and we

had to sink or swim on our own. Big change was needed. Our goal was to create a culture of performance. Almost immediately, we implemented a policy that everyone in the company would have some pay at risk.

Whether you realize it or not, one thing is true in just about any business. You get what you measure and you pay for. When people's jobs and livelihoods depend on something getting done, it almost always gets done. This means it's important to keep score in order to know precisely how the business is doing in each key area, and to hand out rewards to employees when the goals they've given are met. That's why a percentage of everyone's compensation at Imation was based on achieving company goals to do with operating income, cash generation, and revenue. An individual could end up receiving nothing, or achieve as much as 150% of his or her bonus percentage, depending on the results, and how much of that individual's income was at risk. Those in positions that stood to have the largest impact on outcomes had the most to gain or to lose. Bonus levels as a percentage of salary ranged from three percent for hourly and some administrative employees to fifty percent of the CEO's compensation— with most executives above twenty-five percent.

This proved to be a very effective arrangement.

No More Communistic Pay Practices

A peculiar situation developed at many large companies, particularly at very successful companies like 3M, during the last third of the twentieth century. I call it "communistic pay practices." My biggest disappointment at 3M was when I was promoted to manager there—a very important career step. I received a salary-controlled three percent pay raise.

I had to ask myself, "Is this what I work sixty hours a week and travel fifty percent of my time for?" If I'd known then what I know now, I'd still have been disappointed, but I wouldn't have been surprised. Most employees at many big corporations receive the same pay raise each year. If the company-wide increase is going to be three or four percent, you can expect almost everyone to get a raise in that range. You can also expect managers to rate almost all their employees as satisfactory or higher. Let's face it. These rankings simply aren't based on the actual performance or the true contribution an employee has made.

Management has itself to blame for this phenomenon. Most people will look for the least painful path. Conducting business this way allows people to avoid conflict. It constitutes the easy way. All they have to do is treat everyone basically the same, keep them satisfied, or at least content and unafraid, and things will run along without disruption and uncomfortable moments. The problem is, executives and managers are not doing their jobs when they work this way. Companies succeed based on the performance of their best people. These people need to be motivated and recognized so that they will deliver their best. They must feel valued for the contribution they make. Don't kid yourself. The most productive employees know who the unproductive people are, and when it comes to compensation they resent being treated the same. This belittles their achievements and undermines their self-worth. On the other hand, paying for performance and giving recognition of a job well done are two actions that will drive them to achieve even more. In our case, they also represented important elements in our effort to establish a culture that would create and sustain success, which is why we instituted performance ranking and zero raises.

In an effort to spur all our managers to build more productive teams, we raised the levels at which top performers could be paid. Every year, based on our corporate budgets, each manager was given a set amount of salary increase dollars and a set number of stock options. Managers then decided, with consensus reviews and rankings, the raises and options that would go to each team member. Although there was no specified percentage goal, fifteen percent of employees typically received no raise at all, and top performers often earned six, eight or even ten percent raises during years when the corporate-wide average raise was three percent. As part of this process, we, the executives of the company, experienced two years out of six when we received no raise at all.

This put managers in the position of having to explain to employees why they were to receive no raise or stock options when that was the case, and to work with them to help them achieve a higher ranking the next year, or face losing their job or being demoted.

This phenomenon of everyone being satisfactory is, unfortunately, a product of our society today. The attitude has developed that everyone should feel good about themselves. It's an attitude that says all our kids are "above average," which is, of course, impossible. This may be good for short-term self-esteem. Certainly, we all want to believe we are good and that our children are, too, but this kind of wishful thinking can be harmful in that it separates us from reality and may keep us from expending the effort required to improve and thereby reach our true potential.

When practiced, an attitude of acceptance of less than adequate performance creates trouble on any team or in any organization. Performance must be measured, and the top performers rewarded and motivated. Lesser performers must be identified and worked with. If they cannot or will not improve to an acceptable level, they should be let go. This policy is tough for managers to abide by, but it nonetheless should be part of their job. A clear requirement for performance and excellence must cascade from the shareholders to the Board, to the CEO, and to every level throughout the company. This is what sets excellent companies apart from underachievers and eventually will create long term success.

Some employees, managers and executives may be performing very well, some may not. It is the responsibility of managers and supervisors to determine who is and who isn't, and to act accordingly.

It may surprise you to learn that employees responded extremely well to this. The best performers became motivated and felt they'd been recognized when their accomplishments warranted it. The system gave managers the tools to build high-performing teams. Perhaps most important, it forced them to lead rather than to simply manage those in their charge.

Public Recognition

We created a "Top Performer's Award." Rather than just give bonuses and recognition to the sales force, we expanded this practice to include the rest of the company. Each year we would choose top performers who had gone above and beyond what was expected in their jobs to achieve outstanding results. Everyone at Imation had the opportunity to nominate whomever they felt was deserving. Rather than recognize only the winners, we also included spouses and partners, so the impact of what had been achieved would be felt within the family as well as by peers in the company. Recipients came from all different functions, all different levels, and from other countries as well as the United States. We would hold a daytime meeting of the entire headquarters staff, where coffee and ice cream or cake would be served. Winners would be flown in from wherever they lived and worked. We would have a guest speaker, and recipients would then receive their awards in front of this assembly. We also sent out announcements of the Top Performer Award winners, which included a photograph of each and rundown of what accomplishments had led to the award. This practice became so popular and generated such enthusiasm that business units in the different countries began having their own similar award programs in addition to the worldwide program.

Say Adios to Perks

A positive culture is created by more than pay practices and positive recognition. We wanted everyone to pull together for success, for executives to work in the field, roll up their sleeves and get their hands dirty right next to their employees. We wanted them to be visible and involved, rather than aloof and apart. Our goal was for everyone to feel a sense of equality, that they were members of the same team regardless of the titles that followed their names. One way to help create this was to eliminate all perks. Like it our not, executives will always be paid more than other employees. It makes sense they should be paid in proportion to the time they must devote, the risks they must take, and the expectations placed on them concerning what they need to accomplish. But pay is one thing, and perks are another. It works against a healthy atmosphere to set executives apart, or to place them on a pedestal by giving them perks and other special treatment. That's why, as part of our change, we avoided any executive perks. We had no corporate airplanes, no fancy offices, no assigned parking spaces, no limos, and no exotic meeting locations. Our Board meetings were almost always held at our headquarters or at airport hotels in order to make travel easy and convenient.

Employees are not blind. They see what's going on. They watch all the executives closely and determine for themselves if each one is "walking the talk." An example of this came home to me one morning in our parking lot.

As an early-morning person, I usually found a parking place near our headquarters door. But one morning I'd been to a breakfast meeting off site and did not get to the lot until mid-morning. All the parking spots in our front lot were taken except those reserved for customers. I drove around the entire lot, then up the hill to one much farther away. I walked to the office in ten-degree Fahrenheit weather. The truth is, it was no big deal and I thought nothing of it. But during the day two different employees let me know their teams had watched me from their meeting room windows, driving around, looking for a place. They were pleased to see I had not taken a customer spot.

Employees quickly figure out which leaders are personally committed and which are not. They respond to and follow the leaders accordingly. That's why our goal was to create a team at Imation, not stars or prima donnas.

A Push for Urgency

Another culture change we wanted to make was to instill a sense of urgency and to foster a sense of ownership of action plans. To keep it simple, we used the motto, "Do it now!" The fact was, in the businesses we were in sometimes "now" could be late. Customers' technology deadlines had to be met or we would miss out on the business.

An attempt to light a fire under people was another departure from the 3M culture. A practice in place there allowed R&D people to use fifteen percent of their time to work on any creation of their choosing. When asked at Imation if we would have the same policy, my answer was a resounding NO! We simply could not afford this luxury. All our best peoples' time had to be focused on meeting customers' time lines, or we would not survive.

Respect for Everyone

But we did not discard the 3M culture in total. Perhaps the most important direction we took at Imation, one we continue to work on, was to make respect for everyone a top priority. Respect for one another leads to a good working environment. Respect fosters cooperation and facilitates achievement. It also is the perfect catalyst for a workforce that values diversity and strives to gain from everyone's strengths.

For an environment of respect to take hold, it had to be evident from the top down as well as from the bottom up. This is why a key decision we made was to involve people in the difficult changes that had to be accomplished and to do our best to gain their buy-in, or if not their buy-in, at least their understanding. It would have been easier to leave them in the dark on major changes and challenges until the last possible moment, but this would not show them the respect they deserved, which we hoped they would return. So we risked upsetting and discouraging our employees by going public with a number of our divestiture plans. I had faith in our people and believed they would step up and do what was necessary. And you know what? They did. Good employees understand events occur that cause problems, but they do not want to be dictated to by these events. Being open and involving everyone in what must be done maximizes chances for success even in the worst of times. It creates a team, a spirit of "We're in this together. Let's get it done."

This attitude of being honest and up front worked to our advantage in other ways as well. It kept investors behind our company because they could see we were taking necessary actions. It helped us hold onto the confidence of our customers. It was only possible to go public with our plans, however, because our people did not panic. They rose to the challenge again and again, and faced the tough decisions. Being open and frank with them wasn't easy, but it allowed them to become part of the solution—and by trusting our employees, we gained their trust.

Do people like to hear these tough messages? No! Do they get angry at management and the situation? Of course. But if they feel they are being dealt with honestly, treated as professionals, and allowed to work toward a solution, they keep moving forward and make a real difference.

LESSONS LEARNED:

- A company is only as good as the people who make it up, and the leadership focus must be on maximizing their buy-in, focus and performance.
- Communicating and listening to the key people, including them in the decisions and actions, and simply thanking them for their extra efforts make a huge difference.
- Employees come first, and they create the value for customers and shareholders. If management forgets this, they will lose the commitment of their people and will fail.
- Recognition of high achievement and the overcoming of tough challenges is critical. A thank-you handshake, a handwritten note, a phone call—all are incredibly appreciated by employees and motivate them even more so than money. People want to know what they did was recognized and appreciated, not overlooked or unimportant.
- Recognition builds esprit de corps and creates strong personal commitment to success.
- Leaders must be driven by personal commitment. They ought not to "direct," but rather, should lead the way by "walking the talk."

Continued on next page . . .

LESSONS CONTINUED:

- You get what you measure for and pay for.
- Communistic pay practices and entitled programs are to be avoided. Pay for performance.
- Executives belong in the trenches with their teams working in a spirit of mutual commitment. Pay them well, but avoid perks that set them above the team, or create a special category.

Chapter Six: The Role of Communications

Constant and consistent communications was the most important tool we had to overcome fear, and to create optimism and enthusiasm about the future of Imation. Stakeholders, including employees, customers and investors, want to know what decisions are being made, what direction the company is taking, and more than anything, why. Being brought into the loop is what begins to create buy-in and confidence across a company. It can keep customers on board, bring in new investors, and hold onto old ones. It can prod employees out of states of paralysis and get them moving toward solutions. This is why we knew we had to make an aggressive effort to communicate, communicate, communicate.

Brad Allen, our Communications Vice President, was brought in by my CFO and me within two months of the time the spinoff was announced. Brad came from Cray Research, which had just been sold to Silicon Graphics Inc. He also had terrific experience from years at D.E.C., both in that company's halcyon days and later when the value of D.E.C.'s stock was caving in. He brought a good deal to the table and proved to be an incredibly valuable guy to have on board.

There's great value in having an expert like Brad on the team—someone with credibility who has contacts on the Street and experience in developing and nurturing relationships. One of the mistakes a lot of top executives make is not having a strong enough person in the investor relations and communications job. Perhaps this is because they don't know what they're missing. I had a board member once say, for example, when I was fighting for a raise for Brad, that investor relations people are a dime a dozen. You lose one, you go get another. Well, I respectfully disagreed. The Communications VP is often the face of the company, and this is not a place to scrimp. Fortunately, I ended up winning that particular battle. There aren't many in the position who network, who know the investors, who can tell the story articulately. A good communications man or woman can be invaluable by leveling with you concerning what the Street really thinks. One with credibility can set the Street straight when they have it wrong, and are off base. He or she can keep you out of trouble by making sure all the disclosures are done properly. In my opinion, in most companies it's an underpaid, under-appreciated position.

Have a Plan and Work It

What's the best way to approach communications and how do you keep them consistent? How do you make sure you don't let communications slide and end up in the back seat? The answer is simple. Schedule your communications and lay out your programs in a clear cut plan. Employees, investors, and customers must get regular reports on progress and direction so they can see consistency in what you are doing. This will help build confidence. They must come to expect regular communication and get it.

Brad and I identified three constituencies—customers,

employees and shareholders—and put together a plan to communicate with each on a regular basis. Every communication that went out took all three constituencies into consideration. It was essential to consider how a message impacted each, and to be sure that each communication was clear and consistent. Brad and many other talented women and men in our communications department crafted these messages and became the central clearing house in this regard for the entire company, assuring clarity and consistency.

We began our communications effort almost immediately. Dennis Farmer, our VP of Marketing at the time, led this effort along with his team, and they performed extremely well. When the spinoff was first announced we were called Newco. As previously mentioned, we hired Interbrand to help us come up with a name, we asked our people all over the country and the world to volunteer names, and we narrowed them down to three or four. We had focus group interviews and other research conducted and decided on the name Imation. We launched this new name in April even though the spinoff would not be official until July. This gave us some visibility during that six-month period between the announcement and the official launch.

We also sent out introduction letters and brochures to all our customers worldwide. We ran rifle shot ad programs aimed at business to business customers. We used whatever media vehicles would meet our needs, including direct mail, quarterly newsletters, meetings, brown bag lunches with ten to fifteen employees, customer lunches and dinners, and ads in product packages such as diskettes. This culminated in the July 1 launch with events at every Imation location throughout the world.

Diskettes were our most ubiquitous product, so we promoted the company in every box. We were selling more than a billion a year at the time, which meant there was a good chance if someone was using our Matchprint product, or Medical Imaging, or some other Imation product or service, they were also using our diskettes. As a result, we had our own mass media vehicle. During the transition period from November 1995 to July 1996, the outside of the box still displayed only the 3M logo, but we used the inside to pave the way for the change. In addition to enclosing Imation literature, we put the Imation logo on the diskette itself—all part of a carefully orchestrated communications plan.

Advertising was only one of many tactics. I appeared on business programming carried by CNBC and CNN, and gave newspaper and Public Radio interviews. It took about two years before we had enough credibility to get stories in magazines like BusinessWeek. We were always very careful to make this exposure company-oriented, rather than personality-oriented. We wanted to make Imation and its products the stars of the show rather than pump me up as the CEO.

One tactic we used in order to bring everyone in the company into the loop was to send out videos worldwide. For example, my direct reports and I would put together a program and presentations in Oakdale, which included a situation analysis, objectives, and an action plan. We'd have a professional video made of this event and send copies to every Imation location in every country. In this way we made sure everyone got the same message.

Huge meetings are fine for getting out information, but if you want some give and take, you need to have small meetings of ten, fifteen, or maybe twenty people. So we held lots of small group sessions. Few people will ask questions in a large group, and frequently those who do simply like to hear themselves talk. People are more comfortable speaking out in small groups. They're more likely to ask questions and voice concerns, especially if the group is comprised of people in the same area of the business. This is a major reason we organized specific meetings with just R&D people, just manufacturing people, just marketing people, just finance. Individuals feel comfortable in an environment made up of peers. They ask questions such as how a certain action is going to affect them and their department or function. You'll never get those kinds of questions out on the table in a large group. It is important to have both large meetings and small meetings, which provide an opportunity to address what's on people's minds and build their confidence.

Say It Often and Be Consistent

We learned in the early days of birthing an overweight newborn company that it's easy to lose people with mixed messages. Events were happening fast and people's minds were diverted as they passed through a time of mind-boggling change. Confusion causes uncertainty, and it becomes easy to lose sight of goals. This is why repetition and consistency are so important.

An advertising executive once told me about a client for whom he developed a marketing communications campaign. It was a big effort and took about six months of hard work. First there were the briefings by the client and the company's engineers and marketing people. Agency personnel went back to their offices and held brainstorming sessions to come up with ideas. These were refined, brought back, and bounced off the client. Revisions were made and concepts presented. A media schedule was developed. After some back and forth, this was finally approved. The client signed off on everything at each step in this long, drawn out process. The ads, brochures and web pages finally went into production. Photography was taken. Copy was written. Everything was given to the client one last time to approve. Finally, the agency's work was done. The magazine ads and TV spots were in the can. The brochures sent to the printer.

A week later the client called and said it was time to start the process all over again. The ads were getting old.

The ad executive shook his head. "I wasn't sure how to break it to my client," he said. "He might have been tired of the campaign, but the first ad hadn't yet appeared in the media."

It's a fact of life, and perhaps a tough one to live with. If the message is getting boring to you, it's probably just starting to get through to everyone else. In fact, in the case of the story just related, "everyone else" hadn't even seen the message once before the client thought it was old and the time had come to move on to something new. The truth is, you have to keep pounding key messages home in a clear and logical way until you are so sick of them you want to scream. Then pound them home some more.

Timing is Critical

No one other than a few insiders knew about the spin-off before the public announcement. The same was true of other big announcements that came later from Imation, such as divestitures and restructuring. To keep things professional and correct, you can't tell employees this sort of thing before you tell the Street. To do so would be to selectively disclose important information that's likely to have an impact on the stock price, and to risk ending up in the Big House like Martha Stewart. A full blown announcement has to be made. Often this is done in a press conference, or by sending out press releases to the media and the Street. Analyst phone calls are also made on the day of the announcements but after the information is public.

When we were about to make an announcement, everything was carefully orchestrated. We would have it coordinated down to the minute to make sure we kept things legal, but didn't leave our people hanging out to dry. Usually, leaders were told the night before after the markets had closed. They would be given the information they needed to hold meetings at their locations throughout the world. Then a press release would go out before the market opened. The employees would be informed by email within an hour of that. I might also send a voice mail to everyone throughout our system. Employees would be instructed to go to a certain place at a certain time, depending on what time zone they were in. Then the communications meetings would take place. The information would already have been released, but the announcement would be repeated, and employees would have the opportunity to ask questions.

It's important to realize people look to their managers to give them the key messages. It's one thing for the CEO to say it. But most people are more concerned about what the person they report to thinks. After all, he or she is the one who decides whether the person goes or stays, whether they get a raise, and what job assignment will come that person's way. What people want to know is, what does my boss think? We established a system of cascading communications so people heard most messages from their bosses and could ask them questions rather than simply receiving a missive from on high.

Funny how we always seemed to have good attendance at these meetings.

First, Explain "Why"

A restructuring announcement or a divestiture was always a big event, so we had a definitive process we followed. We had to be sure we touched all the bases and didn't lose anyone. A basic rule was everyone had to know where they were in the organization at the end of the day. You see, uncertainty is the biggest barrier to progress, so we would cascade the message down to every manager so he or she could explain the move, why it was needed, and the plan for the future. Everyone needed to see their name on a chart and to know the reasoning behind it being where it was. This encouraged people to get on with their jobs.

Naturally, the spinoff was viewed as bad news by many, as were later divestitures and restructuring. My experience has been that being open with bad news or tough messages is extremely important, because employees will find out about it whether you like it or not. What I've learned is that people can handle it as long as it's given as quickly as possible and in a straight-forward manner. You need to say what has happened, recognize the negative aspects as well as the positive, and say what's going to be done and why. If bad news of any kind is held back, if it's delayed, and people don't understand the implications and what needs to be done, additional problems will almost certainly develop.

It's important to answer as many questions as can be anticipated up front. Otherwise, productivity and morale will suffer. I've seen it happen often. Something happens, or a change is made, management avoids addressing the issue, and people have to catch up. When people don't understand the why of a situation, uncertainty is created. They're left to wonder, where do I fit, why are *they* still here, and why are others gone? People become paralyzed. Progress is frozen. People start hanging around the water coolers and talking. "What does this mean?" they all ask. All kinds of rumors get started.

The best thing to do is to get the why out up front, and answer as many questions as you can. Then, there's less to talk about at the water cooler. Rumors will still circulate, but they are usually bizarre and fewer people will pay attention to them.

A lot of managers make the mistake of being secretive because they think people will stop working if they know, for example, the plant where they work or the job they are doing is going to be eliminated. These managers are wrong. I know from experience it's uncertainty that breeds inaction. This may be counter intuitive, but knowing a plant is going to close will cause the people there to work harder. I know this because we once had a few plants where rumors were rampant we would close them. When we announced we were indeed going to close them, and gave a specific date, performance and productivity picked up significantly. I can only guess the workers at those plants wanted to prove management was wrong in the time they had left.

Here's a specific example. Under 3M in the 1980s, we moved diskette coating from the Camarillo, California, plant to a new coater we put in Weatherford, Oklahoma. People at the Camarillo plant were despondent that we were taking this away from them. Six months was required to make a full transition. During that six months, Camarillo delivered record-low unit costs. We even questioned our decision, but decided we'd made the right one because we had newer and better technology in Oklahoma. The point is, the Camarillo workers wanted to prove us wrong and worked longer and harder to do so.

The lesson was, being up front with bad news is the way to go. That way, people get on with things instead of becoming paralyzed by uncertainty. No one benefits when uncertainty is allowed to exist.

We also learned there is no such thing as a secret. If two people know it, word slips out to the grapevine and people find out. And if they don't find out everything, they will find out just enough to distort it and generate a rumor that may be worse than the truth. So the sooner you get news out, the better off the company and the people will be.

We found when we bet on people's good intentions, rather than constantly guarding against people's bad intentions, we were always better off. Most people want to do what is right. There are only a few malcontents who would throw a monkey wrench into the works. We also found malcontents who go to the press are not listened to. Typically the media does their homework. They usually won't print something that isn't substantiated. They will talk to management and to other employees. The bottom line is, you weather the storm a lot better by being up front.

Honesty Really is the Best Policy

We learned a lot of communications lessons quickly. We were changing so much early on, we learned pretty fast that if you didn't get the people to understand why something was happening, action slowed or stopped. The "why" of the spinoff from 3M, for example, was a tough message, but it was important for people understand it. We needed to be consistent and clear. Explaining it in meetings big and small taught us a valuable lesson.

When you get out in front and communicate, you also

start to get feedback, and you learn what people are thinking and what's important to them. You may quickly realize, as we did at first, that you're not getting the message across.

"Uh-oh, these people don't understand," often was what I was thinking.

We answered the question "Why the spinoff?" every day, over and over again. We had to be consistent. The short answer was, "These businesses do not fit 3M's business model. As a result, 3M cannot focus properly on them, which takes away from their ability to be successful. These businesses make a lot more sense independent of 3M so they can change to meet the needs of the markets they are in."

And that answer was true, even though perhaps it was oversimplified. Frankly, 3M was frustrated with these businesses. What they all had in common was that 3M lost money on them, or they were low performers at best. Clearly, they didn't fit the model. The model 3M had was a fifty percent plus gross margin, and these were thirty percent gross margin businesses, and fifty and thirty don't sleep well together in the same bed. They really created defocus and uncertainty at 3M. Since the people who were spun off to Imation loved 3M, it was important to explain why we were no longer part of that company, and why this was not the end of the world. In fact, it could be a good thing. We were going to move faster, change aggressively and become more responsive to customers.

So, the number one rule in communications we learned was to be open and honest. This extended beyond meetings and announcements. We worked to create an open envi-

ronment with an open door policy. We practiced management by walking around, and this helped.

Almost everyone agrees that being visible and
approachable is important, but this is not something many
executives feel comfortable doing. Nevertheless, you need
to be willing to face and answer the questions in informal
meetings as well as in those that are orchestrated if you
want to create an environment of trust. You are not going
to get the support and effort you want if you just lay out
goals and directions without telling each constituency why
you're doing what you are doing. Don't make the mistake
of thinking they are psychic. Every single individual needs
to understand, and this means they need to be told. It isn't
logical to expect people to follow without first being led
through the rationale.

I believe strongly that the CEO must make most key
change announcements personally. He or she needs to be
on the front line to take any heat and to instill optimism for
the future. This goes for leaders at every level. All must do
their part, starting with the CEO. Responsibility for communications cannot be delegated.

As I conclude this chapter on communications, let me
say I now believe it is impossible to communicate too
much. All three audiences were crucial—employees, customers and shareholders—and they were all anxious to
hear and learn everything they could about the company.
Their uncertainty could not be overestimated. Consistent,
frequent contact at all levels was vital to overcome the situation so that the company could go about the business of
business.

LESSONS LEARNED:

- There is great value in having a top notch communications VP who can develop a plan and work it, develop good relations with the media and the Street, and make sure all the proper disclosures are made.
- Consistent and clear communications to all constituencies are necessary in order to keep them on board and pulling in the right direction.
- Use all the communications tools and vehicles at your disposal, including videos, advertising, meetings, publicity, newsletters, quarterly reports and so forth.
- When you are getting tired of saying it, chances are your message is just beginning to get through.
- Make sure big announcements are timed properly so your people aren't left hanging, but you meet all legal requirements.
- Always answer why. Bringing people into the loop builds loyalty and trust. They will be more productive because of this.
- Be up front with bad news and get it out quickly. Uncertainty breeds paralysis.

Chapter Seven: Customers Come First

One thing is obvious. In any business, customers come first. If you don't have satisfied customers, you won't have a business for long. Our most critical priority as a spinoff company in a tough turnaround situation was to solidify our relations with customers, and to develop deeper positions despite great uncertainty. That's why, beyond creating a new culture, our top priority was to gain customers' confidence and to overcome concerns they might have about Imation's survival. Because of this, I visited key customers and had numerous meetings with them outlining my vision and attempting to project the optimism I truly felt.

One of the rules we adopted was that whenever I traveled, whatever country I was in, I had to see customers every day I was there. I would either go out and call on customers, or we'd have them in for lunch. Or we'd have a customer group dinner.

Every employee needed to understand that the customer must come first, and this was where our focus had to be in order to survive. This didn't mean giving them anything and everything they wanted. It meant selling our value to them and meeting the commitments we made.

It is extremely important when trying to implement change and simultaneously hold onto customers that top executives call on customers directly. They need to be highly visible in the market. Many top executives don't like this role. They don't want to be in the field or to meet customers in sometimes painful negotiations. The fact is, however, this is a critical part of their jobs. They cannot afford to shrink away from it because the company will suffer if they do. Getting out into the market set an example and a tone for all employees and shows the customers they are important.

Know Your Customers' Needs

Customers are the people who use your product. To properly serve them, and to come up with new products, you must know their needs, wants and desires. Top managers need to get out of the office and into end users' locations to really see how a product is being put to work. As CEO, I found it very valuable to meet large users personally, to understand their applications and to give them confidence the entire company was working to support them. Such visits illustrated to customers that their business was valuable and important to us. Personal customer visits helped me learn, and it allowed me to sell the value of Imation.

Bring Customers to You

We also scheduled events for customers as well as for partners and distributors. We knew we were a viable company with value to offer, but realized others had never seen our operation and might have a different image. Our perception of ourselves and their perception of us could well be opposites. I came to the conclusion long ago that no matter what I thought or hoped the perception of the company was, in reality it was probably a lot less. The only way to improve that perception was to force interaction. This meant bringing as many people as possible to the company to see it firsthand.

Early in Imation's history, it seemed our sales people always wanted to have customer events and visits at our factories in warmer climates. We had a factory in Arizona, for example, that may have been the smallest and the least impressive in the company. Nevertheless, it was the most popular in terms of where Imation salespeople wanted to hold customer events, particularly during cold Minnesota winters. We had another plant in Southern California—same thing. One of our best, most dynamic plants was North Dakota. Do you suppose the sales guys wanted to take our customers there? Of course not.

Our corporate headquarters, located in Oakdale, Minnesota, is extremely impressive. It includes a 450,000, state-of-the-art, modern Research and Development Center. Even so, we had to force our people to bring customers to our site. Until they did it enough, they didn't realize the impact it had. When customers turned into the driveway and saw the scope of our operations, they invariably said "Wow!" It took their breath away and instantly transformed perceptions from the idea we were a fly-by-night operation into the realization we were a major player.

"We had no idea how serious a company you are," was a typical comment. That first impression was priceless—certainly better than advertising. It was a lot more effective than visiting a small plant in Arizona, no matter how warm and sunny the climate. So getting both customers and investors to our headquarters became an important priority. Both then realized we had substance.

One more word about this. It shouldn't be totally left up to the sales people and executives to be ambassadors for the company. Everyone must sell the value and work to gain customer and investor confidence. We made a big pitch to all our employees on this subject. Everyone is selling, all the time. Sales isn't just the job of the people with the sample cases knocking on doors, it's every employee's responsibility. After all, this is something that can directly impact their livelihood. The attitude and approach of receptionists, secretaries, customer service representatives, scientists, engineers, and anyone who comes into contact with customers can make a big difference in how people view a company.

Investor Communications

As a new public company, we had a lot to learn, but we had to generate investors and learn on the job. Fortunately Imation had an excellent and experienced Investors Relations Director in Brad Allen.

For every ten shares someone owned of 3M stock they would get one share of Imation tax free as a result of the spinoff. It seemed clear a high percentage of these 3M investors would want to sell Imation. Individuals who'd invested money in 3M tended to be those who wanted stable stocks, which paid a regular dividend. Imation was essentially a start-up company in what could prove to be a volatile situation, and we would not pay a dividend at the outset. As a result, the stock would appeal to a more aggressive investor who was looking for a turnaound and value increase. Also, many mutual funds that would get the stock would be required to sell it because they had bylaws prohibiting them from owning stock that did not pay a dividend. It was clear, only a limited time existed before practically our entire shareholder base would turnover. This made finding new investors a top priority. As a result, we went on the road to gain new shareholders. Present shareholder and prospective investor contacts were made. This effort gained us a strong foothold in the public markets.

We kicked off our Street interaction with a road show. Fortunately for me, I enjoyed this part of my job. Selling investors is like selling any other customer. You must illustrate the value proposition you have for them, and you must be clear, concise and gain their interest and attention.

We educated prospective investors on our company and our opportunities. We outlined a direction we were going to take and how we would create value. We also emphasized the strength of our Board of Directors and governance. It was also critical to illustrate our new, performance culture and our focus on financial discipline.

Know Your Target Investor

We found there's great value in understanding what investors' goals are. For example, are they interested in a company with a turnaround opportunity? Are they quick-turn investors, looking for a fast gain before they get out? Are they long-term investors who seek value creation over time coupled with dividends and financial strength? As in all business endeavors, you must focus on targets that constitute a good fit, those who will value your direction.

I recall once when I was explaining our new product development opportunities to one large investor, he stopped me and said, "Bill, I'm sure all this is exciting and will be important, but what you're talking about here is your job. Tell me how much cash you are generating, where's the lifeblood of the company coming from?"

This fellow wasn't interested in what might be. He was interested in what's happening today. Cash generation from operations is an indication of the basic health of a business and of its ability to take advantage of opportunities.

Continuous communication is crucial to gain and hold investors. You must be consistent with your message and invest time by visiting investors personally. While analysts and their reports are important, most beneficial are the one-on-ones with investors where you get your message out and build the level of interest required for an investor to bet on your plan and your direction.

Be Careful Not to Over Promise

A word of caution is appropriate here. A huge downside to the exciting, heady launch of a new company or a turnaround is that the challenges and difficulties which lie ahead are largely unknown. You have embarked on what is very much like a pioneer expedition. Everyone is excited, a little fearful, but very much full of hope and bravado.

"We are finally free of the barriers to progress imposed by our parent. We will no longer be held back. We are in control of our destiny," may be phrases bandied about the hallways, meeting rooms, and presentations. There are very likely to be exaggerated expectations that this new independence will give a company control of its economic destiny from day one.

Unfortunately, you don't know what's down the new road, or what barriers and challenges will arise unexpectedly. A lot of hard work will be required just to survive and persevere in order to keep the teams on point and on task. And you won't have the security of the parent company's balance sheet and support.

The urge at spin, at creation, is to promise success, be confident, and preach value. And certainly, optimism is important as we've discussed. But the most effective approach for long-term success is to keep expectations as realistic as you can without slipping into a negative assessment. Over promising can lead to disappointment and discouragement among all of your constituencies. Challenges and new realities are certain to present themselves. If the expectations of employees, investors and customers are allowed to run wild, disappointment is going to set in even as successes start to materialize. Once you under deliver to those expectations you will find yourself in a constant battle to recover, even while making strong progress and improvement.

Soberly realistic expectations may not generate as high an initial stock price, but they will lay the groundwork to build momentum step by step and provide room that may be needed to overcome errors of inexperience and unexpected challenges. Realistic expectations allow for small successes to be built upon. Believe me. You may not see where or how, but surprises will come. Not only management, but everyone must be prepared to expect tough times, surprises, and a hard journey before success can be claimed. The advice is to balance enthusiasm and optimism with a healthy dose of realism. Then, the constituencies will more readily accept the tough actions that will need to be taken to move forward and carry out the work that must be done.

Dryview and Superdisk

Our Dryview Medical Imager and Superdisk storage are a couple of examples of how letting optimism get out of hand hurt us. In the early days at Imation, expectations for the Dryview Medical Imager, and for the Superdisk floppy disk replacement ran extremely high. The Dryview Medical Imager produced X-ray films using a dry process thereby eliminating dangerous wet chemicals that emitted fumes and were difficult to handle. The process made X-ray development safer, cleaner and more efficient. Before this process was invented, places that made X-rays in effect were mini chemical plants with all the attendant hazards. Naturally, everyone was enthusiastic about this new product.

Superdisk was a 3.5 inch floppy that was able to store as much data (120 megabytes) as a Zip disk. But it required different hardware than a standard floppy disk drive. This turned out to be the product's downfall.

When it took longer to develop Dryview than expected, and when computer hardware manufacturers did not endorse and support Superdisk as we had hoped and supposed they would, the impact on Imation was far worse than it had to be. Our optimism and enthusiasm resulted in a credibility hole we had to climb out of before we could regain momentum.

Err on the Side of Caution

It's natural to get excited about new direction and new products. Hyping very real opportunities like these can get everyone charged up. Employees buy in and stake their confidence on them. Investors get on board. The problem is, seldom do new opportunities or products follow a rigid time line. They must be created painstakingly, and at times be revisited and redirected if they are to be long-term successes. As the leader, you need to realize this and make sure others realize it, too. Things simply may not work out in the most timely or productive manner. Superdisk was proven to be a great product, but hardware manufacturers bet on other solutions. It's better to paint a conservative picture, or to present a time line that allows room for rework. Then, if you beat the time line or out perform the conservative scenario, you'll be a hero instead of a goat.

People in the financial world often are betting their jobs on you. You outline your goals and expectations. They pick your company. If the results don't follow and fund managers and brokers fail to return the gains to their investors you hoped would be there, they've lost credibility with their customers and you've lost credibility with them. This is why it's so critical to deliver quarter-on-quarter results. It also underlines the wisdom of not over promising or being overly optimistic in public communications. Make sure you highlight the challenges as strongly as you highlight the opportunities that exist.

Be Careful with Analysts

Analysts will continually try to gain more information than what has been published because, like most people, they are always looking for an edge. They will even call down into your organization to see if they can get more insight or data. It's critical the CEO, CFO, and Investor Relations Director tightly control information flow. The rule must be everyone gets it, or no one gets it. You have strong SEC rules and regulations including the Sarbanes Oxley requirements to point to as the reasons no one must be allowed to acquiesce to requests for additional information or non-public data.

This is a critical area to hold firm on. There can be no exceptions. Public communications should be scripted and documented, and the entire organization needs to be trained not to provide more information or to answer questions for anyone other than stating what is already public information.

The Importance of a Top Notch CFO

Your CFO is a major key to relations with the Street. His or her credibility can go a long way toward building investor trust and confidence. For Imation, I hired Robert Edwards, an experienced CFO from Santa Fe Pacific, in 1998, in the middle of our restructuring—after we announced the impending sale of Medical Imaging to Kodak.

Robert is a large man, an imposing gentleman, a smart and experienced guy, who is somewhat introverted. He's a fiscal conservative, likes cash generation, and he led the way for us on value creation priorities. I'll have to say I'm partial to a conservative CFO. He or she is the guardian of the books and the accuracy of our public statements. Nothing is more important than financial discipline and accuracy. I was fortunate Robert and I worked so well together, and I believe this type of relationship and trust is crucial to a good operation.

At the time Robert came to us we had no comptroller and our treasurer was leaving. Robert took this in stride and built an excellent financial team. CFOs are not expected to promote the company but rather to state the facts and illustrate the financial position and progress. Robert did this so well it made my job of promoting the company much easier. I believe when CFOs are the drivers of acquisitions and business development, there is more risk of inaccuracies or of moving too far from the core of your business. An ideal CFO is at the center of financial decisions and investments, and is a devil's advocate on these investments, protecting the financial solvency of the company and its reputation. An optimistic leader and a great partner for me, Robert did an outstanding job in this area. He was credible and consistent, engendering the confidence of our investors. It's important that the CEO and CFO are a close team, in lock step on everything to assure consistency and accuracy. The Investor Relations Director needs to be part of this team and in harmony, also, and the three of them need to convey this to the Street.

The Role of Road Shows

Companies put on road shows to support their stock, for an IPO, or for a new public offering. An investment banker typically sets up visits to large numbers of investors to whom you can present the company's story, plans and goals in the hope of generating interest in buying the stock.

We targeted Value Investors because we were in a turnaround mode. Value Investors are looking for companies they foresee will have dramatically improved financial situations in the coming years. Such companies typically are in a turnaround mode as we were. Today, we target GARP—Growth at Reasonable Price investors. In this case, investors are looking for stock at a reasonable price that they think will grow in value.

In a turnaround situation, as has been mentioned, it's vital to communicate confidence and enthusiasm. It is important to state goals and outline how strong the opportunities for success are. This communication causes employees to have the confidence to hang on and work to survive, and it causes investors and customers to give the company a chance to carry out plans for success. Value Investors are somewhat more stable and consistent in their decisions than pure growth or momentum investors, who sell over shorter time spans to realize a quick return. Nevertheless, they definitely must see a significant upside in the long term price.

Our road show lasted about fifteen days. We had eight to ten presentations per day with additional group lunches and dinners. Many were held in New York, Boston, Baltimore, and Washington. Some were on the west coast, and a number in Minnesota. Usually, it was the CFO, our investor relations manager and me on these calls. I enjoyed this part of my job, and frankly, it is one thing I miss. I like getting out in front and presenting something I believe in to very astute, demanding people. I guess this was my sales experience coming out in me.

Selling a New Culture

It was important to let Value Investors know we were creating a new culture at Imation that was oriented for growth. We described Imation's culture as "performance-based" in that we were moving from an entitlement-based culture to one where performance was critically important not only for an individual's advancement, but also for survival. We outlined the basic components that would foster change and improvement:

- Pay for performance
- Non communistic pay practices
- Customer and cash motivated
- Respect for everyone and valuing diversity
- Build employability, not lifetime employment

Your Board Is a Selling Point and Critical to Success

I was fortunate to be able to put together a solid Board with well-known, successful people, who would be challenging and critical. We outlined our Board to investors at every opportunity, as most investors recognized these individuals and their accomplishments. This helped instill confidence and credibility. Charts in our presentations showed each board member and described the experience he or she brought to the table. It was obvious these were successful people who were not going to let the company get out of control.

An independent and professional Board of Directors will greatly increase your chances for success. This group not only will help guide the company, it will build confidence among shareholders and customers. Our Board members asked a lot of hard questions and frequently challenged us. It would have been easier to have the local fire chief and the police commissioner, or close friends on the Board, but in retrospect we did the right thing for Imation, and the right thing for our investors. Having a strong Board representing them gave them a sense of security that their interests were being protected.

To accomplish this, it was necessary for me to move fast after the spin was announced. We would be more than a two billion dollar public company on July 1, 1996, and I knew we needed a properly-organized Board of Directors. There was no time to waste, and I had no experience with Boards, so I spoke with governance experts and experienced Board members to learn how to go about forming one. I also studied the best practices in U.S. industry.

Contrary to what self-proclaimed governance experts of the post-Enron era would have you believe, I found there has always been a set of solid guidelines for use in this regard. They were simply ignored by some companies.

We embraced the best practices and, with the help of a former 3M executive, Larry Eaton, we set about to build a strong, credible, independent Board of Directors for Imation Corporation.

The quality of being independent came first on the list of criteria. Company knowledge is not necessary or even encouraged. Independence and an unbiased look at the company by experienced business people will uncover issues and opportunities faster and more effectively that scrutiny by those who may have difficulty separating the forest from the trees. We set key policies so that the only insider Board member would be the CEO. We also set age limitations on membership (70), and we worked to get members with the diverse and necessary experiences that would be helpful to a new company.

I was fortunate to gain agreement from Bill George, the very successful CEO of Medtronic Corp in Minnesota, to be on our Board. With his support and endorsement, we built a very credible, experienced and active group of directors. Some of the first to sign on were Daryl White, the just-retired CFO of Compaq, Linda Hart, the CEO of Hart Industries who is also very experienced in governance with a legal background, Marvin Mann, the CEO of Lexmark who led that company out of IBM in a spinoff in the early nineties, and Ron LeMay, the president and COO of Sprint, who has both legal and general management expertise. We also added Mark Pulido, the President and COO of McKesson as well as Larry Eaton, an experienced 3M executive and former leader of these businesses.

By following best practices and networking, we built a truly excellent Board. The members faced unexpected challenges over the years, but stayed the course and helped Imation create success from what in fact was a very uncertain start.

Imation's Board was and is a strong and independent group. We had CEO experience, legal and governance capability, financial expertise, acquisition experience, geographic diversity, international experience and spinoff success. As Chairman & CEO of Imation, I was the only insider Board member. That policy remains in place today.

As the years went by, we added other strong Board members to replace departed ones or to add new experience:

- Michael S. Fields, President, The Fields Group
- Glen Taylor, Chairman of Taylor Corporation and owner and Chairman of the NBA Minnesota Timberwolves
- Richard Belluzzo, former CEO of SGI and President of Microsoft
- White Matthews, former Chief Financial Officer of Ecolab
- Charles Reich, former Executive VP of 3M
- Charles Haggerty, former CEO of Western Digital Corporation

LESSONS LEARNED:

- The corporation must speak as one voice, consistently and accurately.
- Employees must be trained to avoid giving inside information to outsiders and always to refer questions to company communications professionals.
- CEO/CFO relationship is the most important one in the company.
- Profitability drives stock price. As quarterly profits meet expectations the stock price will respond.
- Communicating the downside, the potential challenges as well as the positives, will establish more credibility.
- Employees, customers and investors will cry out for faster progress, success now, and explosive growth. But buying into this without outlining the potential challenges can lead to setbacks that could be avoided with well-planned, longer term milestones.
- Be simple, clear, open, and consistent.
- Have a formal communications plan and work it. Make sure everyone is conveying the same message.
- Create a clearinghouse for any public communications, the CEO's office to start.
- Under promise, over deliver.
- You cannot communicate enough. But try!

LESSONS CONTINUED:

Build a Truly Professional Board:

- Create a Board of independent directors other than the CEO.
- Get experience from as many fields as possible with emphasis on finance and operations.
- Board member experience checklist: Financial expert, public company CEOs, legal expertise, international experience, entrepreneurial spirit, acquisition experience, technology understanding, market and industry understanding.
- Do your best to recruit directors who will be credible to shareholders.
- Use their expertise and advice to guide and teach the company to succeed.

Chapter Eight: Restructuring

As has been mentioned, the 3M business model and structure simply wouldn't work for Imation because of the highly-competitive nature of the industries we were in. Obviously, management sincerely wanted to see the company succeed, but frankly, 3M management had no concept of the scope of change and the amount of cost reduction that would be necessary to position Imation to succeed. This is not surprising. In the beginning, we didn't fully realize it either.

A Realistic Cost Structure

3M was paternalistic and protective of its people. The company's modus operandi was to employ a sizable administrative support staff. This type of structure was a disaster for a low-margin business. Like it or not, an industry determines the gross margin available for R&D (Research & Development) and SG&A (Sales, General and Administrative Costs). 3M was used to working on fifty to sixty percent gross margins but Imation had margins of about half that.

To make the math simple, let's say we sell floppy disks to Office Max or Staples for a dollar each and it costs 70¢ to make one. If we want to make a profit of 10¢, which is certainly not huge, that leaves 20¢ for R&D and SG&A. 3M was in the habit of spending 31¢ to 36¢ for this while still making a profit in the 20¢ range. Clearly, 3M's math didn't add up for Imation. This combined with continuous annual price erosion of ten percent or more a year, as well as short product development cycles, meant something had to give. And it had to give fast.

The cost structure would have to be reduced dramatically at the outset, then be reduced continuously to stay competitive. Imation would have to increase productivity, reduce head count, reduce support costs, and reduce unit costs—all by more than ten percent a year—if we were to succeed. At spinoff, Imation had more than 12,000 employees worldwide, a large percentage of whom were staff and administration as dictated by 3M's corporate model. Sales, general and administrative plus R&D costs were more than 35 percent of sales, totally unaffordable if Imation was to survive in the competitive, low gross margin businesses it inherited. This new entity was simply too big, too costly, and too cumbersome, and much of the needed reduction would have to come in the short term.

In 1997 we had the first restructuring meetings. As mentioned earlier, when we'd spun off, 3M had set the structure and named the executives. At that point, fourteen people reported to me. Two years later, only two of the fourteen remained. There were various reasons for these departures. The traumatic spin from 3M was not right for some. The challenge of restructuring did not entice some others. A career at 3M had prepared almost no one to deal with the huge challenge we faced. At 3M in the 80s and 90s, the sense of entitlement often escalated as one rose higher in the company. At a certain level, it became extremely rare for a person to be downgraded or demoted. I'd always thought I could be fired. But apparently I was not reading the right tea leaves. To give you some inkling, when I'd made general manager—perhaps 150 people in the company were at that level—a group vice president had told me, "Welcome to the peerage of 3M." I didn't really understand what he was talking about until I moved out of Data Storage and took over the more traditional businesses in Austin, Texas. Here many executives had held onto their positions despite poor performance and a grudging reluctance to change. They were in a sense "made men" who had become barriers to progress.

A New Structure

So there we were with a lot of very tough decisions to be made. There's a good deal of anguish when you are cutting so many people, as I'm sure you can imagine. Disappointed employees must be dealt with. Uncertainty runs high among those who remain. Training is necessary to help people operate in a different kind of company than they're used to. We had a long list of issues we had to make a bet on, and I knew we'd have to live with the consequences.

We started with 12,000 employees. As of this writing, Imation has approximately 2,500. About one-half of those who departed left with the various business units that were sold. Even taking that into consideration, though, our staff was reduced by half. This was necessary in order to become a viable public company.

127

Every part of the world of Imation was affected, but Europe is where the biggest change happened. We had more than 4,500 employees in Europe at spinoff. Today, there are less than 300. The business is now highly profitable, and more important than it was pre-spin.

When we restructured, we did not simply cut a percentage of people throughout the organization. We took a careful look at what each person actually did and each organizations' purpose and effectiveness. Our goal was to tie every activity to a business unit that was calling on customers and delivering business. If an activity didn't logically fit into a business unit, this gave us the opportunity to eliminate it as a redundant service. For example, we had corporate engineering that did work for a lot of business units. We eliminated this and made it a policy that whatever engineering a unit needed had to be done by that unit and the unit had to pay for it. We did the same with corporate marketing as well as R&D. The result was, we were able to eliminate a great deal of redundant activity and to focus these activities on the customers served by a business unit.

Identifying redundancies between corporate staff and business unit staff was not difficult, but identifying redundancies within business units was another matter. We hired a gentleman named Jewel Westerman to help us with this. Jewel had a computer-based process that allowed us to outline every single job in the company, including where the job was located and what responsibilities were assigned to it. People were not identified, only the positions people filled. This allowed us to see where activities might exist in more than one place at the same time. Leaders of each organization were questioned about each position and why it was necessary, if overlapping responsibilities could not be reassigned, and if we could afford it. In this way positions were realigned and many eliminated. Then people could be reassigned. Obviously, some were let go because their position had been eliminated.

In this way, we designed a new structure for the company by region and put together a step by step action plan that would bring it into reality. An engineer assigned to me monitored all actions against a time line. Keeping track of every action item was important because it would be impossible to reach our objectives if things didn't happen when promised. The person assigned to this would come to me and let me know as soon as a unit or a department got behind schedule. Then I'd step in to motivate whoever was in charge, encouraging them to get things moving faster.

We reviewed our new direction and objectives. We estimated the cuts we had to make, and the organization we'd need to make the new size work. When we outlined our restructuring plan to our Board, the group was supportive and knew it was a necessity for success, but they did not believe we could accomplish what we had planned in Europe, and certainly not for what we budgeted. But with my long experience in Europe at all levels as well as that of Wenck and Northup, we were able to convince them to approve our plan.

We Announce the Plan

We announced the entire restructuring plan worldwide on the same day. I did it personally with meetings and videos. This was a huge deal. We took a restructuring charge of more than $250 million at the end of 1997. We explained why it was necessary. We answered those "Why?" questions before they were asked so no one left the room wondering. We told people where the company stood, and where it needed to be.

Whenever we announced organizational changes, we did our best to make sure everyone knew where they were in the organization—what box they were in. Great care was taken not to miss any names. If names are missed, a credibility problem quickly develops.

If a person wasn't in a box, he or she was usually told ahead of the organizational meeting. So the first people who learned about the new organization were often those who weren't going to be part of it. Sometimes those who were not going forward with the company would be told at the same time the organizational meeting was being held. We did our best not to leave anyone, going or staying, in a situation of uncertainty.

We worked hard to instill optimism and hope in the new plan. If you ever have to play this role, just remember, sometimes your optimism won't be as high as you would like, but you still have to project it. If you don't have optimism and instill it in others, the plan isn't going to work. You've got to get people to believe. It's important to know who on your team can be optimistic and who can't, and depend on the ones who can. As with any company or business, we had both kinds of people on our management team at spinoff.

It's true those years were anything but a picnic. But divestitures and restructuring were critical to survival and sustainability. In order to win against Japanese competition, we had to structure a lean organization and establish a performance-based culture as well as a sharp focus on our strengths. Over a period of five years, we sold five of our seven major businesses. We reduced warehouses from more than forty to less than ten. We reduced our structure in Europe from sites in twenty-eight countries to sites in six countries. As you can imagine, all this resulted in intense pressure on employees. It required people to be resilient and tough and have the courage to believe and build a new, successful Imation.

A New Company Emerges

In building a new company out of a spinoff and turnaround situation, we had the opportunity to create a whole new business the way we believed one should be for our industries. It was a challenge to change this collection of businesses into a competitive company with a culture that would consistently deliver results in the long term. Motivating and supporting our most passionate employees was critical if we were to survive and be successful. We had to find ways to keep them focused on success while simultaneously driving a new culture and a new business model, and the road was not always straight.

Even today Imation faces enormous price pressures. In June 2004, optical disk prices in the market caved by more than fifty percent. As will be covered in the Epilogue, this required another aggressive reduction in the structure in order to meet competition and remain successful.

In competitive businesses management can never stop driving productivity and getting more out of every dollar invested or spent.

Shareholders demand value growth regardless of the price erosion a company has to deal with. One very clear memory I have from our restructuring at Imation is a communication meeting we held after a tough divestiture and restructuring action. A very solid employee raised his hand and asked if the cutting was over and could he and his co-workers now be assured of their jobs going forward. I always answered questions without hedging. If the answer was "No," I said, "No." It was that simple. Unfortunately, "No" was the tough answer I had to give this fellow. Our jobs are never guaranteed, we earn them every quarter, every year, and we must get better continuously to stay ahead of our competition. We had to ensure all our employees understood this reality and acted accordingly.

Downsizing in Europe

At the very beginning I knew we were overstaffed in Europe. 3M wanted to give me more people than we finally agreed to take so they could reduce even more overhead. We fought this as best we could and still ended up with

Productivity per Employee Continues to Improve

Revenue per employee has steadily increased to $439,000.

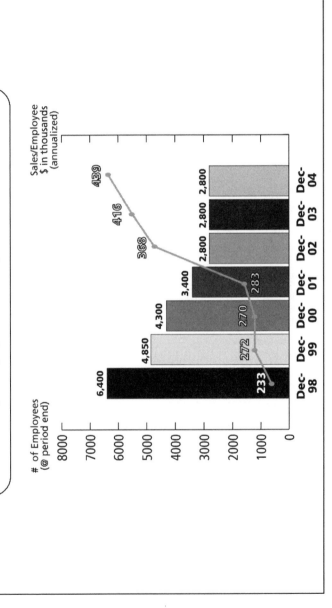

considerably more structure than we wanted or needed. Early on, I went to Europe and visited all the countries. Here's one example of what I found. In Sweden, we had three salesmen out there calling on customers. Believe it or not, there were a hundred people on the support staff in that country. There was no manufacturing in Sweden. It was all in support of these three guys. I remember thinking the shoulders of those salesmen must get very weary from supporting all that infrastructure.

Imation was in twenty-eight countries in Europe with full business structure. I set a target to reduce that to eight countries, and met with my newly-selected leader of Europe, Dick Northrup.

"Dick," I said, "We simply cannot support this structure with our revenue base and our industry's margin levels. I want to reduce the number of locations we have in Europe to eight."

Dick looked at me as if I was delusional.

After he recovered from the initial shock, we had a number of brainstorming sessions on this challenge.

Less than a month later, he called me and said, "Bill, how does six countries sound?"

And that's what we did. We went from a structure that had people on the ground in more than two dozen countries to a streamlined organization that had people physically located in only six.

We reduced European employment from 4500 to 300 over a period of four years, and were able to come in under the budget we'd set for reorganization. We had a detailed plan, and we did not compromise one step. Believe me, many objections were raised along the way. Managers would tell us you can't do this in France, and you can't do that in Germany, "The business will collapse." We had a standard answer when we encountered this, and we used it a lot. It was, "No. We will do it according to plan. We will stay the course." The alternative was not viable.

Some people are amazed when they hear this. "I thought you couldn't fire people in Europe," they will say.

This simply isn't true. It is true restructuring was more difficult in Europe than in the U.S. because we had to deal with a lot of different cultures. What we faced wasn't like one company that needed restructuring, as would have been the case in the States. It was like many different companies located in many different places. Even so, we were able to carry out the program in every country. Looking back on it, I have to say it was a great success. Dick Northup deserves an awful lot of credit, as do leaders like Frank Hill, Dave Ferraresi, Tom Foyer, Armand Maarek, John Neidermire and Joe Gote. They and their teams made the end result happen effectively.

The horror stories you hear about the high cost of letting people go in Europe may be accurate, but they tend to refer to isolated cases. The rules and regulations that lead to these horror stories are only valid for certain individuals. By and large, it's the upper echelon people who are overly expensive to release. It's not the same for everyone across the board. If you work aggressively with the system, you can get done what needs to be done. The work councils and unions want survival. These people are smart and can see the handwriting. They understand the difference between some jobs and no jobs and realize you can't keep them all in a tough situation and still survive. So it's best to attack a European problem head-on, just as you would attack any restructuring necessities. The Europeans will use local situations to their advantage. They will come to American executives and say, "No, you can't do this in our country. We are different." But this isn't true. What is necessary for survival is possible.

Even so, no one believed we could do it. Our Board didn't think it could be done for the amount of money we'd budgeted. But we dealt with the work councils in the countries involved. We were open and clear about our objectives, and why we had to take the actions we put before them. We closed down businesses in certain countries, and it did cost a lot of money. We had to take a large restructuring charge and sizable debt, but we did what we had to do, and we did it under budget.

LESSONS LEARNED:

- Restructuring requires a very detailed, disciplined action plan with a strong engineer or manager to coordinate it. At Imation we had Barry Melchoir and Jack McNamara.
- The restructuring plan must have complete buy in by all leadership.
- The CEO must be on top of the action plan and hold weekly status reviews and action development improvement sessions.
- Your cost structure must be tailored to meet the needs of your Industry. Drastic change is often required to bring this to the place it needs to be.
- Our course of action was right: A restructuring plan was developed and announced worldwide on the same day. We answered all the why questions and let people know where they stood to eliminate as much uncertainty as possible.
- Except for the top echelon, downsizing in Europe isn't a great deal more difficult than in the U.S. You must have a plan, stick to it, and work through local work councils dealing with each different country and culture appropriately.
- People are the most important asset a company has. Their experience, courage and willingness to step up to the challenge will determine success or failure.

Chapter Nine: Financial Discipline

Imation succeeded because we dedicated ourselves to financial discipline and business fundamentals. This may sound simple and logical, but we could easily have gone the other way and bet on growing our way to success. If we had, we would have failed.

Each business we got in the spin naturally wanted the chance to grow, spend and survive. 3M had had the option of closing them down, selling them, or including them in the spin, which was a way for 3M management to avoid difficult, defocusing, disruptive actions. Now the businesses had to survive as part of Imation, or we would be the ones to have to take the tough actions.

I had the leaders of each business unit present their plans to me. Looking back, it's clear most of the plans and budgets I saw were overly optimistic, and it seems obvious they were put together that way to buy time. Here's an important lesson. If I'd been more cynical and critical, I believe we would have saved a year of struggle. What I learned can save you valuable time.

The effort to buy time wasn't the only factor working against us. It's true many were down in the dumps at spin-off because they'd been cut loose from their beloved 3M. But many others who came were not at all forlorn. Quite to the contrary, many regarded this as an opportunity to free themselves of the rules and discipline of 3M, and to invest in their ideas without constraints. It would be a new day—

a time to nurture creative juices. Clearly, an attitude of liberation was in the air, an attitude of having been released from parental control.

Remember when you first arrived at college? The young men and women who came from strict homes and stern parents who had imposed lots of rules and early curfews were often the most likely to cut loose and go wild. It quickly became apparent something similar could happen at Imation. This attitude had to be reined in if we were to succeed. To accomplish this, we decided to develop key financial policies to guide our company:

- Finance is the most important department in the company.
- Finance is the center of all our activity.
- We must focus on the customer and CASH.
- Financial returns must determine our decisions.
- We will measure all our actions.
- We will pay for financial achievement.
- We will follow a strict financial and decision-making process.
- We will establish a business model needed to win, and stick to it.

At spin, people wanted to spend. There was a cry for big advertising budgets, big signs, fancy launches and meetings, new creative development ideas, and new plant investments. These were heady days, and those kinds of expenditures could have killed us. So I made a basic decision, and established our Finance Department and financial fundamentals at the center of the company. This was very different from what had existed at 3M. There, if you ran a business, you might have finance people working for you, but 3M financial people did not report to you. Parallel reporting extended up through the financial organization to the CFO and then the CEO. You might say finance at 3M was a conscience or audit function. One never had the feeling the financial people were really part of the business and invested in it. They oversaw the reporting and cash, of course, but did not always take ownership or always actively participate in running the business.

Stay Focused on the Fundamentals

To remain financially successful and become sustainable, you must build off your core businesses, your core technology, skills and market positions where you have a chance to lead and a strong advantage to help you drive share and cost improvement. We will discuss how to profit from the core of a business in Chapter Twelve. Here, we will focus on business fundamentals.

At Imation we achieved financial success and sustainability by identifying and following strict financial discipline and business fundamentals.

- Focus on building profit from our core.
- Question everything. Evaluate investments and negotiations.
- Never stop reducing costs.

- Look for investments close to our core, utilizing our strengths.
- Build on our experienced people.

Don't Expect to Grow Out of a Hole

Don't fool yourself into thinking you can grow a business out of a difficult financial situation. Growth without strict financial discipline and business fundamentals will not result in profitability. It will result in larger problems. I learned the hard way after the spinoff that you must challenge everything. I learned most plans rely on growth to solve tough problems, and that the most important word in the business dictionary is "No!"

Use Zero-Base Budgeting

In listening for the first time to reviews from leaders of the spun-off businesses, I probably believed fifty to seventy-five percent of what I heard. Often, the details of plans presented were not examined or aggressively challenged. In retrospect, I should have started by believing zero and forced each team to prove every aspect of their plans. My policy should have been zero-base budgeting. In other words, I should have had each business leader work his budget up from zero revenue rather than adjusting from the other direction, which often included unrealistic growth projections. GE does a good job at this. We learned as we moved forward and used companies like GE as benchmarks, but it cost us time, energy and a lot of indigestion.

Question Everything

My advice is to attack every plan and be aggressive and stringent in all reviews. It's not easy to strike a balance between a hard-nosed position and projecting the optimism needed to keep people up beat and confident. Nevertheless, a hard-nosed position is necessary when plans and budgets are presented. People who have to go through it hate the process, but it is necessary because it works and will speed up a turnaround. This is the reason we made financial analysis the center of all our decisions, and this made for an easier, more straightforward process to separate what was real from what was pie in the sky.

A Cost or an Investment?

Here's a question you must always ask. Is it a cost or an investment? The key to effective cost reduction is to determine whether something is a cost—which may be nice to have—or an investment—critical to success coupled with an expected dollar return. In a turnaround situation, or in a very competitive market, it is crucial that costs be cut to the bone. No "nice to have" spending can be allowed. ROI (Return on Investment) must rule the day or the competitors will pass you by in efficiency and have better costs with which to attack you with on price.

We always explained what costs we could not afford and the steps we needed to take to bring these costs in line. We put a great deal of emphasis on whether something was an investment or a cost. For example, entertaining ourselves. Does that bring a return? Of course not. How about limousines and private jets? Or flying first class? Or, for example, why do we have a a bunch of different marketing companies selling their wares to the company? How does that help us sell more product? Just because you as a marketer like a particular ad firm does not justify having to duplicate efforts and pay twice for them. If we consolidate, we can get better deals. So lets consolidate.

Getting Rid of the Frills

An example of "nice to have" was when I took over the Austin, Texas group for 3M. There was corporate jet service from St. Paul, Minnesota, to Austin and back three times a week. It was a convenient way to go to meetings in St. Paul headquarters, and it saved time for the twelve people on the plane each day. But it was a luxury we could not afford if we were to turn around profitability. It also in effect encouraged people to take unnecessary trips to the headquarters. Our challenges were not in St. Paul. They were at our Texas location, around the country, and around the world.

One of the most unpopular decisions I've ever made (but one of the easiest) was to scuttle that shuttle. The very next quarter our trips to St. Paul went down by forty percent. So we not only reduced costs, we increased productivity. I became known as "the Grinch who stole the shuttle," but it was the right thing to do.

In principle, I'm against corporate jets. They are an

executive perk that insulates executives from the real world of commerce. I believe executives need to travel with their sales people, to see the market first hand, and stay in touch with reality. Private aircraft and limos set executives apart and reduce effectiveness and hands-on time. They remove executives from their team and place them far from the customer, their field people, and an understanding of their needs.

People Don't Have to Like What They Hear

We didn't always expect our constituencies to agree with all the rationale or like the actions we took. When we announced a change in medical coverage, for example, we took the medical programs of the ten top companies in Minnesota including 3M, Medtronic, and others. We pegged our program right in the middle at number five. The problem was, 3M had a very positive program that was far ahead of number two. The gap between where we had been and our new program was significant. And that's what people looked at and thought about. They didn't care if what we were providing was better than Medtronic, Honeywell, or whomever.

If people are strongly against what is being done, they leave if they are an employee, or sell the stock if they are an investor, but at least they have the information they need to make this decision. Our experience showed, however, if you really provided the "why," people tended to give the strategy or direction a chance and usually ended up buying in. But if you dictate and don't explain, you end up in a painful situation, often with a loss of credibility and with many uncertain and indecisive people whose productivity is going to plummet. Being open and honest with all information is the simplest and most effective way to get the organization moving in a positive direction.

Just Say No

In my opinion, "No" is the most important word in an executive's vocabulary. It is easy and even fun to say yes and encourage a direction, or a new program. But too often when this happens resources are spent on a poor opportunity for return. Of course you will want to take great care not to miss an opportunity. But remember, there are always going to be enthusiastic champions for a "Yes" decision. Few will be recommending no. But let me say from experience, seldom have I ever regretted a no answer. By putting every initiative, business and investment through a very rigorous, unbiased financial test, you weed out the pipe dreams, the "flavors of the month," and get down to the company's core—the areas where strengths, experience and market position can lead to success.

Fully-considered "No" decisions of all kinds strengthen a company. Say no to the bad customer who only wants price exceptions that will hurt you. Say no to a new development idea that may be exciting to R&D but lacks enthusiastic customer backing or need. Say no to creative ideas that have little basis for financial return and are not close to your core competencies that would insure successful implementation.

The Why of Cost Reduction

At Imation, our businesses were in industries where the customers and competition allowed 30% gross margins, moving toward 25%. To achieve 10% operating income, and to invest in our future, we would have only 20% of sales dollars to pay for all non-manufacturing costs. This included sales, marketing, finance, human resources, legal, IT (Information Technology), sites, security, Board of Directors costs, and R&D. That meant 14% to 10% SG&A and 6 to 4% R&D costs. This was a tough target, but for our survival it would be necessary to reach it. The industry necessity set the tone for continuous operations improvement.

	Imation at Spin	Financial Objective
Gross Margin	35%	25%
SG&A	29%	10%
R&D	7.5%	5%
Op Income	-1.5%	10%

The How of Cost Reduction and The "Dream Goal"

We set hard targets that may have seemed to some to border on the impossible. I've learned almost no target is impossible, but you do have to find the right formula and get creative on saving versus spending. I learned this lesson at 3M.

Many of us at Imation had been part of the Data Storage Division and the diskette business at 3M. In the mid-eighties we were called upon to turn that division from break-even to strong growth and profit generation. The 3M CEO supported our efforts, even though the targets we set were intimidating. In 1985 the diskette business generated more than a hundred million in revenue and lost almost thirty million because price erosion ran wild and unit costs were high.

We set our turnaround targets and took them to our Group VP for approval. We had a three year target to take unit costs from $1.25 per diskette to 50¢ per diskette. Our VP declared that a losing scenario and sent us back to find more cost reductions. We returned after much work with a 32¢ unit cost within three years. He said we were in the right direction but we had it inverted. It needed to be 23¢.

Everyone felt that was a nearly impossible goal, but we took it on. Reaching it meant survival and success. And you know what? We achieved it! We hit 23¢ per diskette three years and six months from that day. We also created high growth and a profitable business during those years, going from huge losses on a $100 million business to double-digit profitability on a $300 million-plus business.

The Group VP had moved on to other jobs by the time we hit 23¢, but even so, I thought he might be interested in our success. I called him and gave him the news.

His response? "You were six months late."

We learned you must set very aggressive goals, goals you do not yet know how you will reach, if you are to win in a very competitive business. We experienced 17% price erosion per year during the late eighties and early nineties on diskettes, but achieved higher levels of cost reduction due to fantastic manufacturing productivity gains, product design, and creative sales and marketing programs.

The dream goal, stretching the enterprise, is critical to a turnaround success. It forces you to make the tough moves that deliver success.

We Drive Down Costs

At Imation, we started with 28+% SG&A costs and 7+% R&D. We drove these costs to 13% SG&A and 5% R&D, cutting our cost structure almost in half in order to survive and create profitability. This drove financial success and investor return.

Productivity increase and cost cutting as tools cannot be overemphasized. It is vital in a competitive market, so efforts in this regard must be relentless and continuous. We achieved nine percent profit on revenues in 2002 and sustained that level for more than two years. We held head count at 2800 for the total period while Data Storage sales grew at double digit rates each year. This was possible because we were able to reduce unit costs to keep up with competitive price erosion, and our people continued to increase productivity.

Cost reductions can never stop. This effort must be relentless. Solid growth helps offset price erosion but, unfortunately, in a tech environment you can never be lean enough. You either make reductions annually or take a large, structural cut every few years. The realities of competition make it necessary to drive leaner, more efficient operations and drive productivity continuously.

Everyone in the organization must be constantly on the alert for better ways to do business and for cost reduction opportunities. They must be looking for ways to do more business with fewer resources. This is vital for survival and success and must be institutionalized across every part of the company. Every job in a business can contribute to increased productivity, creative use of resources, and therefore cash and profit increases.

Cash is King

No enterprise can succeed without cash generation. You either earn cash or you borrow it to pay for your operations. Debt puts off the inevitable and creates a higher financial mountain to climb. I realize, of course, some debt is positive. The right amount enables added investment for growth and makes sense when the returns are higher than the cost of borrowing. But to a new enterprise or a turnaround, CASH is the blood flowing through its veins. Without it the operation seizes up and ceases to function.

On Christmas Eve, 1997, members of my financial team came to my door and shuffled into my office. They pushed an appointed spokesperson to the front of the group.

"Bill," the spokesperson said, "it looks as though we're not going to make payroll in January."

I felt my brow furrow. "And a Merry Christmas to you, too," I thought. Then I said, "We will make payroll. We will not run a company that misses payroll and doesn't take care of its employees." From that moment, I took a lot more ownership of cash management and raised the profile and focus on cash throughout the company.

As it turned out, we had considerably more cash available than we had first determined because we were in the middle of so much change. We were, after all, a two-billion-dollar-plus company making sales and collecting accounts receivables every day. Even so, the jolt I received that Christmas Eve brought home to me the importance of a cash mentality in a company or business, particularly during a turnaround.

Coming from a large, successful hundred year old company like 3M, cash was never something we worried about at the operating division level. 3M was, after all, an incredible cash generator. Cash was always available so long as the investment was justified, and long term investments were made frequently, with the corporation fronting the cost. At Imation, however, it had to be pay as you go. There were no 3M coffers to fall back on. We had to take on more debt to restructure the company for survival. The massive restructuring we went through required mountains of cash, as did investing in new products. Dryview Medical Imagers, Digital Proofing, and Advanced Tape Storage, for example, were projects we had in the works that required funding. As a result, generating cash became a priority. Our corporate theme became "Customers and Cash." In the early days, a total of 40% of our bonuses were based on cash generation. This worked. It made everyone sit up, take notice, and act aggressively.

Aligning a Bonus Incentive Plan with Needs and Objectives

The plan from day one was to pay for performance—to set goals and tie the compensation of individuals to the achievement of those goals. The only question was how to do it. At first we fell into the trap of the day, measuring EVA (Economic Value Added) and paying on that. In simple terms, EVA is a way to measure economic profit that many feel is more accurate than simply looking at the bottom line, or EPS (Earnings Per Share). In contrast to book earnings, EVA subtracts a charge for the use of all capital—equity as well as debt. So EVA deducts not just the interest on debt everyone can see, but also an invisible charge for the use of equity capital—i.e., the shareholder funds—to recognize that shareholders too expect and deserve a return that compensates them for bearing risk. Unlike EPS, EVA doesn't begin to count profit until the shareholders receive a minimum acceptable return on their investment. In this way, retained earnings are no longer a free form of finance.

EVA may be an important tool for sophisticated investors to use to compare the performance of companies, but calculating bonuses based on it was a mistake. Most people in the company did not understand EVA and how it related to their jobs and activities. What we wanted more than anything at the beginning was every employee contributing to cash generation and conservation. So we changed the metric from EVA to the amount of actual

CASH generated. This was something everyone quickly understood. As Ben Franklin wrote more than two centuries ago, a penny saved is a penny earned, so if you spent less, you generate cash. If you increase productivity, you generate cash. If you reduce capital expense, you conserve cash. If you work only on financially sound projects, you generate CASH.

Everyone soon got the message. If we reached our cash target, we got a bonus. This gave us clear and straightforward goals and unambiguous actions to achieve them.

As previously mentioned, in our plan, everyone in the company had some portion of their pay in a performance bonus. The more a person was in a position to affect the bottom line, the more that person's pay was tied to performance. For hourly workers, it was three percent. For the CEO, it was fifty percent.

We made it clear to just about everyone in the company how they could impact cash and profit. All people needed to do was ask themselves questions such as, how much do I spend on meetings, supplies, advertising, or any activity in the company that requires someone to write a check? How can I economize? Operating income is the most important cash lever so it took top priority. If we did not make our operating income goal, no bonus would be paid. We all became aligned behind the goal very quickly.

Everyone except the CEO and the CFO, who were totally corporate, had some percentage of their bonus incentive based on the performance of the business unit they were part of. The rest was based on the success of the corporation as a whole. Usually, the split was seventy percent for their business unit and thirty percent corporate. This put focus on what people could control.

We also varied the mix of cash generation and other factors from one year to the next based what was needed most during a given year. For example, one year we determined yields should be a top priority. Yield has to do with how much raw material becomes finished product as it passes through manufacturing. If you can get yield up, you not only save on raw materials, you make better use of machine capacity. By cutting down on waste, you are using the machines you have more efficiently and may be able to avoid having to buy additional machines or expand a plant. So generating higher yields saves money on raw materials, produces more product for the same cost, and conserves capital at the same time. The result is improved operating income and cash in the bank.

Yield goals varied by products based on what we thought could and must be achieved. That year, the plants had seventy percent of their bonus based on yield results, and thirty percent on overall corporate performance.

We Learn from Installing IT

When Imation was spun off from 3M, we had no IT (Information Technology) systems, and we had to get off 3M systems for legal reasons within eighteen months. We also had no IT department. Setting up a company structure simply in order to operate and report accurately was a huge challenge. But people stepped up, moved out of their comfort zones and took on this challenge. Dave Mell, a lifetime 3M engineer and general manager, volunteered to lead this effort. He built a team of dedicated people who had to learn as they went along but were committed to getting the job done. People like Colleen Willhite, Jack McNamara, Debra Retenwald, and Barry Melchior came out of manufacturing to take on the challenge. We also had many logistics people, like John Neidermire, Carl Broberg, and Bob Hibbard, who stepped up.

It was a monumental task. We installed a worldwide Oracle ERP2 and created an IT Department in parallel, attempting to keep financial discipline as a critical focus. But we did make some big mistakes. Primarily, we used too much consulting support, and we allowed our businesses to create too many exceptions to the Oracle system we had agreed upon. This cost us dearly because every exception cost us money in programming dollars. Nevertheless, we stayed the course and came live worldwide without damaging our company or hurting any customers. An investment in 1997 of almost a hundred million dollars was required to put a worldwide IT structure in place. Much of what was needed had to be developed inside because Oracle did not yet provide all that was called for. It took eighteen painful months, but the effort succeeded due to the brute force and tenacity of a very dedicated team from all segments of our company.

We learned a huge lesson. As callous as it may seem, when an IT system or process is changed, management and IT must become dictators. A menu for people to choose from cannot be offered. To do so is to create a big black hole for cash to be sucked into. All choices have to be designed by experienced IT people with solid business and management guidance. Most important of all, no exceptions can be allowed.

We put what we learned into practice the next time we had a major IT change. This time we upgraded to Oracle's IIi, also worldwide, with a much tighter process and more strictly imposed financial discipline. Rather than change Oracle's system, we adjusted our processes to fit it. The choice we provided was simple. Either people trained to use the new screens and systems, or they moved aside.

This time we achieved the goal with no consulting. We hired our own IT people, and we came up on time and on budget while keeping customers served and reporting accurate.

The Distraction of High Tech Bubble

Our CFO, Robert Edwards, had been a key leader in restructuring, and we assigned IT to his organization. This was the dotcom boom time, and we were a meat and potatoes organization—not sexy at all. The pressure was on to hire a high-powered CIO to help companies build "Solutions Businesses" and E-business capability. There was a hue and cry to "Spend on consultants, bring in the latest, leading-edge technology and be part of the boom or bubble."

Well, we came down on the side of conservative financial discipline. Robert and I could see only uncontrolled spending in the eyes of the CIO candidates we interviewed. So we decided to tend to our knitting and stay inside with a proven down-to-earth, nuts-and-bolts director of IT, Bob Hibbard. We never regretted this. Bob and his team built a solid worldwide system on budget, and we cut IT costs from six percent of sales to less than three percent. As of this writing, Imation has a goal to get down to two percent or less as margins get even tighter.

We survived just fine through the bubble and the resulting tech collapse because we took a financially disciplined approach to the exciting initiative of the day or flavors of the month. Everywhere companies were diving into E-businesses as if using the Internet was a business in itself instead of just a tool to help get business done. We kept our investment small and used the Net to facilitate our business, not change our business. We may have missed some opportunities, but we protected our company and focus while we kept our turnaround on track.

Operating in a Spendthrift Atmosphere

We were trying to develop financial discipline while the High Tech Bubble was going on all around us. The atmosphere and mentality this dotcom boom created didn't help. Companies were spending lavishly on IT systems, and the future was said to be all E-business driven. As a company, you were ridiculed by Wall Street and others if you didn't jump on board. Naturally, we had executives who wanted to go full throttle into the E-business solutions model, even without experienced people in place. They would have us believe we'd be left behind.

It seemed as though everything was out of sync during

the dotcom boom. Huge gains were being made and the money had to be invested somewhere. Venture firms and Wall Street were dumping big sums on almost any idea, and here we were using financial fundamentals in a hard struggle to survive. This approach was somewhat out of favor. Yet we knew we were on more solid ground than many other high tech businesses that enjoyed huge stock prices but had little or no sales and plenty of losses. I thought the world had gone crazy.

Then solid companies started paying big premiums for dotcom and high tech firms that were mostly smoke and mirrors. Market caps were huge, so paying four or five billion dollars for a company with five hundred million or less in sales was not infrequent. Some of our executives became frustrated seeing the astronomical stock prices out there and they wanted to get in "play." Their idea was to make acquisitions that took us from manufacturing and sales to more of a tech-Internet company since, apparently, that's where the money was.

Nevertheless, we did not buy into areas that had no real sales or were mostly smoke and mirrors. Our mind set of financial discipline helped carry us through, although we did put our toes in the water with a few limited initiatives. And mistakes. Thank goodness, we were careful not to bet the company on unproven opportunities. As we will discuss shortly, we always asked the key questions: Is it real? Can we win? Is it worth it? This kept us from making a lot of mistakes even as we were learning on the fly.

The Solution Sales Initiative

One of the initiatives to get us into the dotcom arena was Solution Sales. This business unit provided companies with solutions when they needed or felt it would be advantageous to move stored data from one medium to another. What we found, however, was there wasn't any real customer pull for this.

One of the problems that caused Solution Sales to fail, I believe, is that we were primarily a business selling data storage media. If we had a solution where storage could be moved from one medium to another, inevitably our customers wanted it for free. People expected these types of services for free or almost free in the dotcom era, and we didn't believe in free. Our philosophy was simple. If you give it for free today, people aren't going to believe it's worth fifty dollars tomorrow. Giving it away is just digging yourself a hole you will not work out of.

Also, most companies that have succeeded big time in the solutions business are huge companies that are offering broad product lines. The products they are offering are methodologies of doing business, including processes and software, with thousands and thousands of employees supporting them. IBM is an example. EDS (Electronic Data Systems) is another. Those are the companies that have won in the solutions software business. Growing it from scratch was a pipe dream, and there were lots of pipe dreams going on during the dotcom era.

For example, one of our executives wanted us to

acquire a firm in storage software that had a market value of five hundred million dollars and sales of less than a million dollars per quarter. He pitched the value of their software and their position as a technology player. I considered it ridiculous, as did my CFO, and we passed on this opportunity. The turndown was received very negatively by that executive and some of his people, but it turned out to be a prudent decision. Today the business in question still has less than a million dollars in sales per quarter. And guess what the stock is worth? It's valued at well under a dollar per share, an infinitesimal percentage of its former trading price. It we had spent five hundred million to buy it, we'd have been betting the company, and we would have lost. We dodged this bullet due to financial discipline and by sticking to fundamentals. Return on investment, cash flow, sales volume proved much more important in the long run than Internet position or dotcom opportunities.

Ultimately, it became clear that, while the Internet is an extremely powerful tool that creates opportunities, it is not often a business opportunity in and of itself. It must be part of a much broader business and customer value proposition.

Always Ask These Three Questions

There can be no doubt financial discipline saved us from huge mistakes. If the ROI (Return on Investment) wasn't clear, we would not go there. We didn't invest in market cap. We believed we must invest in building immediate value, selling real products.

We believed in considering every investment carefully

by asking and answering three questions:

- Is it real?
- Can we win?
- Is it worth it?

The data must lead to a yes answer for all three. We learned this process long ago at 3M. It was developed by a business analyst of the 1970s named Schrello.

Many opportunities to acquire a business or to develop a new product came our way. These might might look promising at the outset. For instance, potential customers might like the product. In this case we could answer yes to the question, "Is it real?" Indeed, there was a market for it.

The product or service had to be something we could pull off with our resources and assets. Did we have the capability? If the answer was yes we had the expertise to design and build it and the distribution channels needed to bring it to market, it moved to the next question.

The most important criteria was always what the return would be. Perhaps the market liked the product but was not willing to pay enough for us to make a reasonable margin on it. In this case, it wasn't worth our while to go forward. While it may well have been a flashy and exciting idea, without a significant financial return, why waste time and money executing it? To do so would pull our assets and people away from other opportunities or our core businesses.

Two Examples Where the Payoff Wasn't Real

A team of marketers came up with a product that would transfer data from one type of memory to another and make it portable. We called the product Ripgo.

Ripgo was real in that the product worked and customers in focus groups like the application.

We thought we could win as it was a data storage product and could be sold through our present distribution.

It failed because it was just not worth it. Customers were not willing to pay $149 for Ripgo, which would have provided a reasonable margin. In the end, we found that $49 was the maximum a broad market was willing to pay, and we could not make money at this price.

We lost a substantial sum on this opportunity, but we stopped the bleeding before we were badly affected.

WE ALSO looked hard at the acquisition of a company that was in our business. We believed that a well-known brand name that would be part of the deal would give us a large boost in markets where our brand was not well known.

The business was real. They were positioned well. We thought we could win with it because it gave us two brands to take to market, giving us strength where we were weak. But in the end, we concluded the acquisition wasn't worth what we would have to pay. During the negotiations the price rose to a point where we would be unable to recover our cost of capital. It climbed so high we finally said, "Enough," and made the tough decision to walk away from the deal. This was the right decision. The process worked as it was supposed to. Our financial analysis said, "No, it's not worth it."

We have not regretted that decision.

Choose Your Best Shots

In any company you must have ongoing development initiatives in order to fuel your future. At the spinoff of Imation, 3M had many projects going on. Those requiring the greatest investments were Digital Matchprint Proofing, Dryview X-ray technology, Superdisk, and four-color, one-pass printing.

People in R&D often believe all initiatives are critical and must be funded. With unlimited cash, perhaps this can be done. In Imation's condition, however, it was critical investments be prioritized and that tough exit decisions be made in order to focus on programs with the highest potential.

As a result, we closed the new coater, "Shodokan," in Japan even before the spinoff was official. We could see the return on investment would never meet what was needed in our business.

We sold the four-color printing project, saving the company the sixteen million dollars per year it took to fund that project. This technology is still not in the market.

We exited write-once optical. This technology has never really succeeded in the storage industry.

We cut back on digital proofing since this was going to be a smaller business in a smaller market than the analog technology (Matchprint®) it would replace.

We killed barium ferrite development for tape storage in favor of metal particulate technology. This was a tough move that took four years to complete but was a critical part of our turnaround.

All this was done because we used a disciplined approach to investments and asked those three simple questions.

The Exabyte Case History

One example of using these questions that worked to our benefit was our investment in Exabyte, a tape drive company. The company manufactured drives in the low-cost user market in the price range of about a thousand dollars each. Their product was excellent, and there appeared to be good potential in new products coming down the pike. Exabyte was in financial straits, however, and the company's survival was in doubt. When we looked at this opportunity, we saw a new management team that was financially disciplined, trying hard to affect a turnaround. What they needed was cash.

We had the cash, and we also felt we needed to have tape products in this market segment, which at the time we weren't supplying.

So, the answer to the first question was yes. The market was real.

Could we win?

Yes, we were already positioned in the market, but we weren't supplying tape for the Exabyte product.

Was it worth it?

We did an in-depth analysis of our two companies and the fit they would make, determined our short and long-range return on investment, and came up with a "Yes." We made the investment, and it has been successful since day one.

The Exabyte deal was a winner for us because it was an opportunity that complemented our core business. We clearly could win in this arena due to our market coverage. And, most importantly, it would bring a financial return that justified our investment.

Perhaps for more than any other reason, Imation survived and was successful because of our heavy emphasis on financial discipline. We never reached a state of perfection or succeeded at every level, of course, but improvement continues because finance resides at the center of all activity.

LESSONS LEARNED:

- Set what look like impossible goals and work back to what you must do to achieve them.
- Don't take on the "flavor of the month." Stick to financial fundamentals.
- Cost reduction is a continuous requirement.
- Determine if spending is a cost or an investment with an ROI.
- Eliminate costs, eliminate "nice to have." It makes the company competitive.
- Challenge everything. Employees will always have rationale as to why spending or structure is necessary. Don't always accept the rationale. Tie all spending to a result.
- Structure your business or company to succeed in your industry and versus your toughest competition.
- Benchmark the best, most productive companies in the world and try to match or exceed them.
- Always ask three questions: Is it real? Can we win? Is it worth it?
- Move on to something else unless the answer to each is "Yes."

Chapter Ten: The Art and Science of Negotiation

We were fortunate as we built Imation into a successful business to meet Dan and John Shulman, Minneapolis attorneys who helped us settle major lawsuits favorably. Dan Shulman, the father of John, is an extremely aggressive and effective litigator who never saw a fight he didn't relish. To give you an idea how effective he and John are, one of the stipulations by the other side in a case they settled in our favor was perhaps the greatest compliment that can be paid a lawyer. Neither could ever enter into litigation against that company in the future.

John Shulman is a gregarious and a very articulate guy, who is extremely credible with all audiences. He is an expert in negotiations. John and Dan are both Harvard Law School grads. These fellows introduced us to Alignor, a very effective interest-based negotiation process Imation still uses today. We will touch on some of the aspects of Alignor here, and if you decide you want to know more, check out http://www.alignor.com. If sales, important decisions, or negotiations fall into your area of responsibility, you won't be sorry.

The Alignor process is an interest-based approach to decision-making, strategy development for negotiations, and for improving important business relationships. It's built on a simple reality. People make decisions based on their own interests. The key to successful negotiating is finding creative and effective ways of satisfying those interests—theirs, while meeting yours as well. The process has become a critical part of Imation's planning, opportunity assessment, decision making and action plan development. We found Alignor so valuable it became a cornerstone of Imation's operations, augmenting our financial discipline. It was an efficient way to insure we addressed all possibilities and all interests in a negotiation, or when a big decision was to be made. Time and again, the data-driven discussion it required brought our entire team onto the same page, and into agreement on how to proceed, which is particularly important in negotiations. An opposing team can often tell when members of your team do not agree and can use the differences of opinion to their advantage. The old saying, "United we stand, divided we fall," is true.

We employed Alignor extensively in many key negotiations, including key account negotiations, lawsuits, our joint venture negotiations with Moser Baer on optical disks, our acquisition of a competitor's assets, and our investment in Exabyte. The issues that arose were predicted in our Alignor interest analysis, and we experienced a positive result in each case.

In fact, Alignor has achieved such successful results in negotiations at Imation and with other companies that the Harvard Program on Negotiation uses Alignor in its pioneering work on Middle East peace negotiations. John Shulman has worked with Harvard Law School Professor Robert Mnookin in dialogue among Israeli leaders about the withdrawal of settlements from Gaza and the West Bank.

How Alignor Works

Alignor involves a three-step process. First is to determine who on the other side is involved and what do they need. This is called "stakeholder interest identification." Second is to determine what can be done to get them what they need so that our side can get what we want. Third is to develop a plan concerning what to do if no agreement is reached. Alignor employs software to lead a team through this process in the development of an action plan or to make a decision. The goal is to take full advantage of the knowledge and experience of every team member as this relates to the issue at hand.

Say you are going to enter into negotiations to acquire a business. People in your company from different departments, such as marketing, sales, finance, R&D, customer service, and manufacturing, will likely be able to provide different perspectives on the business you are thinking of acquiring, and how the acquisition will affect your business. I've seen it happen many times. We get people together, we go around the room, and we find very different points of view. The legal people think one thing. The marketing people another. The financial people a third. Each views a situation from his or her unique perspective. So you not only factor in these diverse viewpoints, you see where they are aligned. As the process unfolds, you are able to document them. That's why it makes sense to have someone from each department on the team. Every angle will be considered.

The Alignor Process in Action

Let's say, for example, you're prepared to the go to the mat on a lawsuit. The procedure would be to get everybody together in a room who knows anything about the facts. The entire process from start to finish takes about a day. All of the interests we have on our side, and all of the issues we have, will be drawn from the group. Then the group will do its best to come up with all of the issues and interests the other side may have. At this point, you need to determine where parties are aligned and where they are opposed. This exercise takes advantage of the perspective, experience, and information of each team member. All of it becomes part of the mix and receives consideration. In this way, the company does not fall into the trap of relying on just one individual's experience, judgment or perceptions.

Alignor helps map out where you want to go. Such questions as, "What can we do to get them what they need?" are answered. Drawing upon the knowledge and creativity of the entire team, different ways of satisfying interests are identified. For example, you may be trying to negotiate a contract for raw materials or parts and there's a price the supplier simply isn't going to go below. Even so, you might need a lower price, so the team would brainstorm options. You might decide to offer to them a longer-term contract, or an attractive benefit in some other area of the business, or part of the country. The objective in this case is to meet their financial needs and still get what your company wants and needs out of the deal.

You brainstorm and evaluate the effects different actions will have on each stakeholder. You consider packages of actions that might include things you don't like but could still make sense as part of an overall package that on balance is good for you. Eventually, once you have it all out on the table, you are in position to develop a proposal. Then you will be able to build trust with your negotiating counterparts by laying out and agreeing on their interests and your interests. You may be surprised how fast concurrence will be reached on these. Your counterparts will quickly and readily relate to their interests, including some they may not yet have focused on. It will quickly become clear to them what they will have to give up if an agreement isn't reached, and this can be very powerful.

Fighting Alternatives

What happens if there is no resolution? This is when you resort to your fighting alternatives. Stakeholders will try to satisfy their own interests unilaterally. They may even try to harm the interests of others. The consequences of each alternative need to be evaluated and the effects of the fighting alternatives respectfully communicated.

Here's an example. The management of a company we were negotiating with decided on the first day they didn't like our deal because they thought we were making too much money. So they demanded a fifty percent price cut if we wanted to do business with them on future products. Period. It looked like a complete impasse. We felt we might as well pack up and go home, but we did an Alignor analysis on the problem instead. We lined up the issues and the interests of both companies to see if we could determine a successful outcome.

Our interest analysis indicated we had a lot of things they needed and wanted beyond price decreases. After going through the exercise, we realized we had a strong position, and our problem was with their top management. We came to the conclusion I had to get out of the way since I was the CEO of Imation and my involvement would force their top management to remain involved and possibly intransigent. If I stepped out of the negotiations, it would be logical for us to work directly with their operations people. Since they were close to operational issues, they were in position to understand the full impact of the other advantages Imation offered. The result was, I turned over the negotiations to our Chief Operating Officer, Frank Russomano.

Since Frank led operations, he was able to work with the operating management at the other company and keep them involved. Their interests were different from those of top management, who were worried solely about price. The operations people had some significant challenges on their plates, such as making sure all products worked and that products in development were ready when they needed to be. Sometimes top management tends to assume this sort of thing will be taken care of without giving much thought to how it will happen. The new contacts in operations were at a level where they realized they needed our intellectual property in order to insure their goals were accomplished.

The situation was difficult to be sure. Negotiations were tricky for the entire time. Even so, Frank and his contacts were able to come to an agreement that included some price advantages and sidestepped the drastic price reductions that would have damaged our company. We were able to do so because our interest analysis gave us strong hot buttons to push. It also helped us develop fighting alternatives, so that if we weren't successful, we knew what we were going to do. Our approach was to make sure Frank's contacts knew what our alternatives were and what we planned to do if negotiations didn't bear fruit. The involvement of our entire team through the Alignor process allowed us to outline all our value to the customer. As a result, we were able to come to a solid agreement that met both companies' interests and got a product to market on time.

The people we were dealing with were very smart. They quickly saw how serious the situation was, and they did what was necessary to help find a resolution we could both live with. Since we understood their interests, we were able to work with them in a cooperative manner. Cooperation created resolution.

Eliminate Chance

Imagine the benefit, for example, of using this process to prepare for a sales call. You'll think through (in advance) everyone's interests, including the critical needs of various players inside the account. You'll also know exactly how your products and services can satisfy those customer needs. When the salesman makes that call, he will be backed by the best information and ammunition possible. This takes chance out of the equation. As a manager you always hope you've got your best salesman making the call, one who is quick on his feet and able to think like the customer. The Alignor Process ensures that the proposal he or she offers will be specifically tailored to meet that customer's critical needs. The point is, the process can be used for everything from negotiating lawsuits, acquisitions, or supplier contracts to field sales calls and customer service. Whenever your people negotiate (which is most of the time), they should use the Alignor Process. For Imation, it has become a way of doing business.

Know When to Walk

You may go through the Alignor process and find, when all is said and done, you don't have much of anything the other business wants. You are much better off knowing this sooner than later. Since you have no bargaining chips, you can quickly move on to something else and not waste your time or theirs. Armed with this knowledge, you won't end up doing a bad deal because you hate walking away from the table. As I'm certain you know, it goes against some people's nature to give up easily. They figure some part of a deal is better than no deal at all. My experience shows it's possible to be terribly wrong about this. Let's face it, it's human nature for people not to walk away from something they think they want. They hang on too long, and take a lesser deal. Later, when reality sets in, they have regrets.

So Alignor can put reality in focus and tell you when to throw in the towel. The way we do it is to figure out our best case negotiation outcome first and then agree on our bottom line. If the deal would take us below our bottom line, we won't take it. Instead, we'll move on. Simple as that. The best part is we don't have to guess or play games about where that bottom line should be. With the Alignor process, our bottom line is clear. Our bottom line is where we can better satisfy all of our interests by walking away than by doing the deal.

Once we figure out who all the stakeholders are and what their interests are, it is easy for us to evaluate any proposed deal by how effectively those interests will be satisfied. This gives us a clear strategy and establishes in advance when the deal will no longer be of benefit. This is done in an organized and disciplined fashion so the data is there to refer to when you are done with the process. It doesn't take long, and let me tell you, you will likely be way ahead of the other side when you walk into the room.

Be the Side with an Advantage

From my experience, I would say that most negotiations consist of acting and reacting because people don't have issues thought out and a strategy laid down ahead of time. At some point in this action-reaction process, a conclusion is reached. Every now and then, people dig in and get difficult as a negotiating tactic to wear you down. These are often competitive negotiators, who are clever enough to try to stay one step ahead of you. Whether you are dealing with an act-react type or a more difficult negotiator, the Alignor process will keep you strategic so that you can get what you want. It's hard to stay strategic during the give-and-take of negotiations if you don't have a disciplined, process-driven approach. In fact, I'd say very few negotiators are truly strategic in that they take the interests of both parties into consideration. Alignor will put you in this top group because it keeps you focused on finding ways to satisfy the interests of both parties.

There's no question about it, people make decisions based upon satisfying their own interests. In using the Alignor process many times, I've found that the more you focus on the other person's interests, the more likely you are to get what you want! You know before you walk into the room what you will probably have to do to satisfy the other side, and once you've done that, go home with your objectives met. The key is to find the best way for the other guy to get what he's looking for in exchange for what you're trying to achieve. You see, a win-win match up is what you're after. Once you find that, success will follow.

Alignor's three-step process is captured in the worksheet on the page that follows this one. It is a disciplined, fast and very effective process that your people can employ using this worksheet, or with simple software tools.

Printing & Publishing Case History

Before accepting or rejecting a deal, you first need to understand how the proposal and the alternatives satisfy or harm everybody's critical interests. This way, when you go in, you know if you don't make things work, they are likely to take such and such an action. You have to ask yourself, can I live with that?

When we sold our Printing & Publishing business, I

The Alignor® Process Worksheet

Step 1: Interests Analysis

STAKEHOLDERS

ISSUES

Step 2: Brainstorm Possible ACTIONS

_____

_____

_____

_____

_____

_____

_____

Step 3: Understand "FIGHTING ALTERNATIVES"

_____

_____

_____

_____

_____

_____

_____

came to the conclusion that if worse came to worst, we had to give them the business. You read that right, *give* it to them. Keeping the business would have been a mistake because of the direction the printing and publishing industry was headed. In short, we could not afford for this deal to slip away.

A little background will be helpful. As you will learn in the next chapter, the sale of Medical Imaging is what made us solvent. When we were in the process of negotiating that deal, we found we could also sell Printing & Publishing right then if we wanted, and get a pretty good price for it. We even had discussions with a couple of CEOs. But after careful consideration, we decided we needed the cash P&P was generating. It was taking a long time to complete the sale of Medical Imaging. Data Storage still required a lot of work before it would be turned around, and our need for cash in the meantime was critical. P&P was delivering the cash, due to our Matchprint franchise, so we made a conscious decision to use it as a cash cow, even though we knew it might be more difficult to sell the business later.

We could see P&P's industry was going digital, and that at some point in the not too distant future, the sales volume and the margins simply wouldn't be there. The handwriting was clear. The coming digital environment would have an extremely negative effect on P&P's operating income. This was because the margins for digital proofing materials and supplies were so much smaller than analog (Matchprint) margins. Plus, with analog, there were many more materials to be sold, including both the film and the chemicals needed to process the film. With our Matchprint® brand, we had a differentiated position with solid margins above forty percent. But all this was headed into the history books as digital took over. In the digital world people think everything should be free. Margins were headed down to twenty percent while the amount of materials used would shrink by one to two-thirds. So a digital sale to a customer was one-third what it had been in the analog days and the margins on that smaller sale were less than half. It didn't take a genius to figure out the industry was going to continue to consolidate and margins would continue to shrink.

This scenario played out during 2001, over the course of the year we were in the process of selling the business. Central to these negotiations was our General Counsel, John Sullivan, who coordinated with John Shulman to use Alignor to facilitate a process to help us maximize our value. The industry was indeed consolidating and what appeared would be one of the survivors, KPG, wanted P&P. In effect they would be buying market share and position as well as digital technology.

In 2000 we made about $47 million in operating income from P&P. As 2001 unfolded and negotiations with KPG went forward, profit shrank in every quarter. Every time we got together with KPG, we had to lower our price. We breathed a sigh of relief at the end of 2001 when we finally closed the deal. The selling price was a lot less than it had started out to be at the beginning of the year, but no wonder. In 2001, P&P made only $19 million for the entire year, and with none of that coming in the fourth quarter. If push had come to shove, we may have been forced to take even less. We'd concluded in our Alignor analysis it was more important for us to get rid of that business than it was for KPG to buy it. Why? It would cost a lot of money to shut it down because of plant closings and severance and asset write offs.

As you might suspect, KPG got the business for a very good price. But even though we could have gotten much more for the business if we had sold it sooner, we had no regrets. We got the positive cash flow we needed from this business during a critical time. And selling the business, even for a bargain price, was better than closing it. In that case, everyone who worked for Imation's business would have been out of a job. By selling to KPG, a majority of jobs were salvaged at least for a time. Many people went over to KPG, then found other jobs and left that company. But at least they found jobs on their own terms, which was better than having to do so while they were out of work. Many employees also found very positive positions at KPG where they could continue to use their skills and experience.

Another Case History

Another example of this process is how we used it to determine the interests of three different stakeholders in our development of a joint venture with Moser Baer.

Moser Baer is an optical disk manufacturer in India. We'd been purchasing all our disks from one of their competitors in Taiwan. After eighteen months of negotiating with the Taiwanese, we knew we would never achieve more than a buy-sell relationship with them. Nevertheless, we had decided we needed a closer manufacturing relationship and more of a partner in optical disks.

One of our marketers brought us the possibility of a joint venture with Moser Baer. We evaluated that company and found state of the art manufacturing and management that also needed partners. Due to very diverse cultures, the negotiations took a while—almost a year. We finally reached an agreement that blended our optical intellectual property and marketing and sales expertise with their manufacturing strength. This joint venture is still relatively new at this writing. It should have the effect of increasing both our businesses and establishing a franchise partnership in the industry.

Moser Baer would not be able, however, to handle all of our needs and we didn't want to lose our alternative source of supply, so we also outlined the interests of the Taiwanese. We wanted to avoid having them attack us in the market. We analyzed what action they were likely to take if the agreement with Moser Baer came to fruition, and established a contingency plan based on our Alignor analysis. Specific action steps were developed, which we executed when we closed the deal.

This planning and consideration kept our relationship with the Taiwanese intact. By using the Alignor process we came to an understanding of their interests. It was this that allowed us to develop plans to communicate and deal with them in such a way that the damage was minimal.

LESSONS LEARNED:

• Alignor is a valuable tool for use in preparing for negotiations and other business decisions. It involves a process that identifies and aligns the interests of all parties involved so that these can be used to optimum advantage.

• The Alignor process can tell you in advance when a point has been reached when further negotiation will not be to your advantage.

• The Alignor process identifies "fighting alternatives" that can put you steps ahead of the other side.

• The Alignor process can help you reach "win-win" quickly.

• Training your management and sales team in a disciplined process maximizes the chance for success and helps avoid losing deals.

Chapter Eleven: Becoming Solvent

One of the low points of the time I spent at Imation was when the financial team came to me at the end of 1997, distressed about the need for cash due to the massive restructuring we were going through. As you recall, they believed we could actually miss making our payroll in January of '98. In my gut, I believed this had to be inexperience speaking. We had a two-plus billion dollar company and were selling product every day worldwide, generating cash. It was clear we had to manage it better, and we needed to conserve cash until we restructured the company more favorably. I got personally involved in cash management, and our team identified ample cash to see us through. We put even stricter controls on cash outflow, but this spurred me to keep looking for a way to get more cash into the business to put Imation on a solid footing from which it could grow.

A Match up in Medical Imaging

Kodak was a strong competitor in the medical imaging business and had better coverage of the market than we did. Kodak had invested large sums of money on technology that would create X-rays without the use of messy and potentially dangerous liquid chemicals. Even so, the company had failed to deliver that product. On the other hand, while still part of 3M, we had spent a similar amount and had been successful.

Kodak had the market coverage we lacked, and we had the product they badly needed to create success. It made sense to get together and we did. They showed a strong interest in buying this business. I looked at this as the start of focusing the company and as a way to achieve financial solvency. We had so much debt and so little cash, and I knew we needed to deal with the situation urgently if we were to survive. Financial strength would be needed to move the company forward.

The Situation with Medical Imaging

The traditional products in Medical Imaging had been losing money. Our coverage of the market was not good. We had a gem in Dryview but we didn't have the market position to take full advantage of it. It looked like selling Medical Imaging to Kodak might allow us to turn around financially. Kodak wanted the technology, had the market coverage, and the scale and scope to launch this new product and profit from it in a big way. We didn't.

Kodak came to us first. We'd met their top executives at a trade show in late 1997. They wanted to see if we could do something together on Dryview, but they weren't interested in buying the company at that time. We were looking at what we could do with Dryview. After a couple of meetings, we realized they weren't going have a dry film product any time soon. We were fortunate to have very good patents that positioned us extremely well competitively.

Things Get Off to a Bad Start

Negotiations got off to a rocky start. We were fierce competitors, and it is always difficult to sit with your enemy and negotiate. For example, our respective views on the value of the business were very different. Perhaps our newness as a company led Kodak to believe they could take advantage of the situation.

Kodak made a big presentation to us, and said they had calculated the business was worth $100 million.

I said, "That's very interesting. You did your analysis. We did ours, too. And we think the business is worth a billion dollars. I'd say, we're pretty far apart."

The truth is, I didn't really think it was worth that, but I did think it was worth a heckuva lot more than $100 million. So, later, the negotiator for Kodak and I got together one on one, and he made a final offer.

He started out by saying, "This deal makes a lot of sense for both of us."

I had to admit, he was right. We needed the money. They needed the product. We weren't going to be able to do with the product what they could do with it.

"Our offer is five hundred and ten million dollars," he said. "We won't discuss another figure."

"Okay," I said. "I'll think about it."

Negotiations Get Tense

We got together again a week later.

I said, "We're willing to do a deal for five hundred and ten million, but it won't be a penny less. We will walk on any reduction of the offer." We owed it to our shareholders to get a fair return and we were going to hold tough to our position.

We ended up negotiating that deal from February, when he and I agreed on the price, until Thanksgiving. We closed on the Tuesday after Thanksgiving. Negotiations took that long for a number of reasons. We were selling one business out of our company so separating it and its assets from the rest was complex. We were also a recent spinoff of 3M, who had joint ownership with us of some patents and some pension responsibilities. We needed to meld three companies' interests to get a deal everyone would agree to.

Another problem was Y2K looming ahead. Kodak wanted all kinds of ridiculous protections in case this happened or that happened. Our position was that no one knew what was going to happen in Y2K and that we were not going to give concessions that would benefit them if Y2K turned out not to be a problem. That would be ridiculous.

There were all-night meetings. We'd sit in separate rooms for four or five hours at a time. It was all part of the game negotiations often become with lawyers from both sides trying to gain a small edge. Fortunately, we had a strong team from our legal and finance departments, from mergers and acquisitions led by Jim Wales, and we had excellent outside counsel from Cravath.

It seemed as though Kodak wanted to drag things out forever, but we knew they could not. We could see they had a deadline coming up, a big trade show at which they needed to announce they now had the Dryview technology. The show would end on Tuesday night, and so they had to finalize the deal before then—at least we figured that was the breaking point.

Later, we learned they had a press conference called for five o'clock on Tuesday. At 4:45 their side came into the meeting room where we were waiting. Their VP of Finance stepped forward and said, "If you will give us your word you'll make things good if something goes wrong with Y2K, then we've got a deal."

Our intentions had always been to support a fair deal, so we agreed. We had built up a lot of mutual respect with the Kodak team, and this became an important factor for both of us at closing. We signed the papers, which took about five minutes, the deal was done. Patience had won the day.

Kodak announced the deal at five o'clock.

We got more than $600 million in cash from this transaction. The sale price was $510 million but there were other things that changed hands such as inventories and accounts receivables that brought the amount up to that. Now Imation was not only solvent, but on very solid ground financially.

A Turning Point Is Reached

The sale of Medical Imaging was a major turning point in the life of the company. Restructuring had taken us part of the way, but to be a sustainable, viable company we had needed to increase our cash position and reduce our debt.

Going forward, other businesses with uncertain futures needed to be divested, of course, but the sale of Medical Imaging made us healthy and our people benefited, too. For example, former 3M leaders like Mike McQuade held our Medical Imaging business together while we carried out the divestiture and ended up with excellent positions at Kodak. Now we had the ability to concentrate on our strategy of focusing on the creation of sustainable value.

We Go Public with Our Divestiture Plan

Although we couldn't announce specifically we were going to consolidate our company in one or two businesses, I wanted to announce we indeed had plans to focus the company much more sharply to create a growth platform for the future. Just about everyone urged me not to announce this, including the Board of Directors, as they felt it would create too much uncertainty for our employees. Nevertheless, I believed it was critical to announce our direction and felt strongly if we didn't go public we were going to lose the Street. We had built up a good investor following. They knew we had to continue to make changes if we were going to succeed and were anxious to learn what we were going to do to create profitable growth.

The reasons people said not to go public were that it would kill morale and make people uncertain and difficult to manage. But I believed our people were stronger and had the courage to manage the situation. I trusted them and believed they trusted management.

So we announced we were going to divest some parts

of the company. Anyone who was alert could easily figure out what we were going to sell. This led to KPG coming and looking at the Printing & Publishing business. Others in the industry looked at it, too. But KPG really saw a valuable fit.

Other Businesses Are Sold

We also sold the CD Rom business along the way. This was a duplicating business, which meant we duplicated CDs for businesses that needed them in large quantities such as for software or music. We had no competitive edge, nothing that set us apart, which meant the only way to compete was on price. The bottom line was, we simply could not make money in this cutthroat business. Joe Phillips and Ron Zinke led this divestiture and saved our company substantial sums.

Then, in 2001, we completed our consolidation by selling Printing & Publishing. Focusing our company was critical for Imation's future success. It helped us develop sustainability. Many very talented people from Imation played crucial roles in creating this focus, including Paul Zeller, Tom Foyer, and Luc Janssen from Finance, our merger and acquisition operators, Joe Phillips and Jim Wales, our lawyers, John Sullivan, Joe Gote, Eric Levinson, John Thomas and many, many others on the Imation team. Their experience and 24-hour, seven-days-a-week dedication made the deals happen. We used key outside help from Bain & Company, including Sharad Rastogi, Darrell Rigby and Bob Bechek. Good outside law firms also provided excellent support.

Implementing our strategic direction of creating our corporate focus required nothing less than a full team effort. We ended up using different bankers in each deal.

Investment Bankers Are Not Always Your Friends

Let me interject a word here about investment bankers. They can be very helpful in rounding up potential buyers and setting the stage for a transaction to take place. Their contacts and networks are invaluable and they know deals. Beyond using them for that, however, we never got too cozy. We would negotiate a set fee in almost every case. In the case of Printing & Publishing, we had a percentage with a minimum and a cap. What we gained from this tactic was that we used whichever investment banker best fit our strategy, we switched when it made sense, and we kept the percentage taken by an investment banker as reasonable as possible. We stayed in control of our destiny and decision-making process. What we lost was that many investment bankers would not follow our company's stock since we were not strong customers of theirs. These two things are not supposed to be tied together, but the reality in the past was there was little motivation to follow a company our size without a more permanent relationship. Clearly, during the bubble and even after, if you weren't doing deals with an investment banker, they wouldn't put an analyst on your business. But we survived not having these analysts follow our company. We just didn't believe the price was worth losing our flexibility and independence.

LESSONS LEARNED:

- Because of a strong position in a market, a technology you own can be worth more to your competitor than it is to you. This was the case with Dryview and Kodak.
- It made sense to sell Dryview and Medical Imaging in order to become solvent and focus our company for the future.
- Identifying our interests and the other company's interests allowed us to negotiate on a level field with Kodak and get what we needed out of the deal.
- Being open and clear with our employees on the challenges we faced and possible actions we might take kept their loyalty and support in place.

Cash and a Strong Balance Sheet

I believe it's a good thing cash generation and strong balance sheets are back in favor by investors. Dividends are also a positive sign for the Street that a company is solid and expects to keep generating positive cash flow.

I have mentioned elsewhere in this book that "bankers are not your friends." Investment bankers are looking for ways to spend your money, the next deal, and not always the right investments. Lenders always want to lend you money if you don't need it, but restrictions and covenants can get extremely tight when you are in need during a turnaround.

Most spinoffs wind up with large amounts of debt as part of the financial agreement with the parent, or for restructuring. When turning around a company or managing a spinoff with a debt load, it's critical that management and not the banks make the decisions. For this reason, you must choose your banking partners carefully, and do everything possible to generate as much cash you can from operations in order to provide leverage when dealing with them.

We experienced an example of the value of cash in controlling your destiny when Imation was passing through its most difficult financial hour. We were closing in on our Medical Imaging business sale to Kodak but we were not there yet. Moreover, we were in very high risk of blowing our covenants as we implemented our massive restructuring. Our debt was more than $400 million and cash availability was well below $100 million. In looking for banks to step in and replace our line of credit, which would expire in six months, we received a very aggressive proposal from one large banker. They convinced me their proposal was worthy of being presented to our Board as an option for their consideration, particularly as we did not have many options. Naively, I agreed to allow them to present it at the Board meeting. To my great embarrassment, the bankers used this opportunity to try for an end run, proposing a completely different version of the debt agreement than I had concurred with. The arrangement they proposed would have put them more in the driver's seat for the next year. As you can imagine, this was probably my most embarrassing moment as CEO of Imation. Fortunately, having an experienced and savvy Board carried the day. My Audit Chairman, while listening to the bank's proposal, stopped them when they put their new spin on things, and said, "Just a minute, gentlemen. I have heard proposals like this in the past, but the presenter always had the courtesy to wear a mask and carry a gun."

His point was made, and we eliminated that option immediately. The Board was patient and supportive during this tough period, and we closed on the Medical Imaging deal two months later, brought in more than $600 million in cash and were on our way to a sustainable future.

The importance of cash generation and availability to controlling your own destiny cannot be emphasized enough. The CFO must be relentless in driving for and conserving cash. The operations people will assure needed investments and positive opportunities are brought forward and considered, and the CEO will call these shots. But the CFO must provide a consistent conscience in financial discipline, spending control and cash generation.

# # #

SG&A Expense* Ratio Continues to Decline

Selling, General and Administrative expenses have declined from 27.6% of Revenue in 1998 to 13.2% of Revenue in Q1 2004

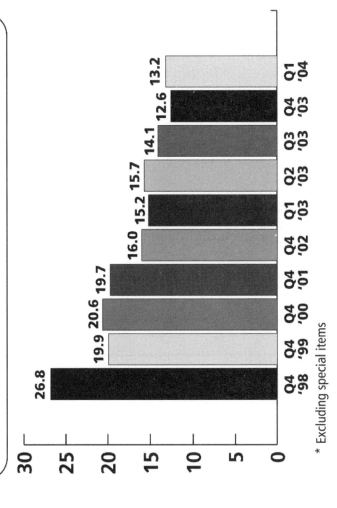

* Excluding special items

imation A Spin-Off from 3M (Data Storage, Imaging & Photo)

	1996/97	Q1, 2004
Revenue	$2.4 Billion	$1.350 Billion
Employees	12,500	2,500
Businesses	7	2
Growth	0	10-15%
Debt	$429MM	0
Cash	$29MM	$440MM
SG&A	29%	13%
O.I.	0	9.9%
Stock Price	<$20	$40

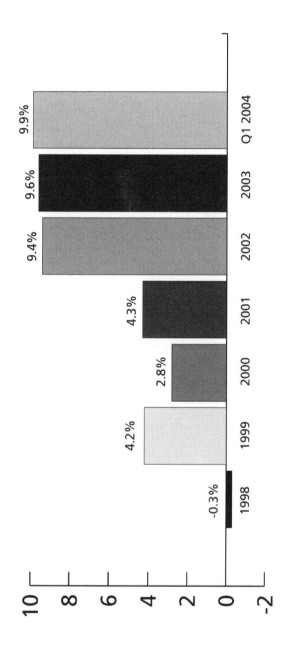

Operating Income %
(Excluding Special Items)

1998: -0.3%
1999: 4.2%
2000: 2.8%
2001: 4.3%
2002: 9.4%
2003: 9.6%
Q1 2004: 9.9%

Chapter Twelve: Focus on the Core

At Imation in the beginning, we were grasping for ways to get healthy. As mentioned previously, many in the company felt a sense of liberation. They had dreams of being able to create new businesses, and of being able to invest in their ideas. But all too often these ideas, while exciting, were too far afield of Imation's competency and assets to have real value for the company. As we pushed forward through tough times, employees looked for new ideas, silver bullets that would propel us to success. We were careful, but even so we tried a few of these with poor results, and they distracted from the critical priorities that would determine our success.

We Turn to *Profit from the Core*

To help us avoid these excursions in favor of sticking to our core to improve our returns and sustainability, we enlisted Bain & Company, a business consulting firm the management of which wrote a book called *Profit from the Core.* This book provides excellent examples and presents powerful data on truly successful companies which built themselves on core business platforms usually developed inside the company, rather than through acquisition. The data the book presents show a large majority of the most successful companies during the last fifty years have achieved their status because they stuck to their core competencies. When these companies did make acquisitions, the successful ones were almost always tied closely to the acquirer's core business, dovetailing with the company's competencies. Acquisitions that failed tended to be those far afield of the core, or in altogether unrelated businesses. I suggest you read this book for the details. Take it from me, you are likely to become a believer because the facts it presents are difficult to dispute and lay out a very compelling direction for any company, and most particularly, for a turnaround.

A Core Is Best Viewed from the Inside

The core of a business can be defined from two different perspectives. In *Profit from the Core* by Chris Zook, a short discussion on three car rental companies brings this into focus: Enterprise Rent-A-Car, Alamo Rent a Car, and Avis. All are clearly in what most people would define as the car rental business. This involves purchasing and managing fleets, running automated reservation centers, managing a branch network, and serving customers who rent cars for various purposes. Within this framework, however, these particular companies have core businesses that are quite different.

Enterprise has seventy percent of the market for insurance replacement and repair rentals. The company got its start in this distinct segment, building its suburban locations and business model to meet the needs of body shops and insurance companies.

Alamo's core business comes from leisure renters, who

don't mind having to pick up rental cars at locations some distance from an airport terminal. The company situates its branches in popular vacation destinations such as Orlando.

Avis's core is airport rentals to people traveling on business. It sells heavily to corporate renters requiring speedy service, newer cars, a variety of business amenities, and, obviously, a network of prime airport locations, most having their cars located within walking distance of the terminal.

Enterprise, Alamo and Avis each no doubt views its core differently, and each is right in doing so. Yet each participates in the rental car business that to the casual observer looks the same.

Defining Your Core Business

So how do you define your core? It's defined by that set of products, customer segments, and technologies with which the greatest competitive advantage can be built. To do this, simply identify:

- Your most potentially profitable, franchise customers
- Your most differentiated and strategic capabilities
- Your most critical product offerings
- Your most important channels
- Any other critical strategic assets that contribute to the above (such as patents, brand name, position at a control point in a network).

Why Data Storage Was Our Best Bet

Profit from the Core guided us to create a clear focus on what Imation had to be to achieve sustainable success. We said no to far-afield opportunities, divested businesses where we were missing key strengths, and focused on where we could win and continue to drive costs down in order to stay competitive. Data Storage emerged as the business we should bet on because it was in the most promising market. As a segment of the information technology arena, the industry was growing. As more and more data is created, more and more data must be stored. We thought we could be a leader in selling that storage. We had the best market position in this business. More than fifty percent of our business was outside of the U.S., so we were strong around the world. We didn't have all the products we needed, but we felt we had the technology to develop those products. Our technical people were good, and we thought we could catch up. Clearly, the Data Storage market offered Imation the best opportunity for long term success and financial return.

In summary, three criteria were used in our analysis to determine the business we would establish as the core of Imation. We wanted a business:

That had real, organic market growth opportunity.

Where we had a strong technology position, experience and a strong intellectual property position.

Where the opportunity was truly global and where we were positioned to win.

WE HAD distinctly different positions in our three biggest businesses, Medical Imaging, Printing and Publishing and Data Storage. Medical Imaging had a great new product, Dryview Imaging, but had very poor market coverage in Asia, Europe (except Italy), and in large segments of the U.S.

In Printing & Publishing, we had a rapidly declining analog proofing business and a very low profit digital business as its replacement.

In Data Storage, we had strong worldwide share, in fact stronger outside the U.S. than in. We had good basic technology, even though we were behind the technology cycle. Most important, the market had a good long term upside as the Internet made more and more data available and easily accessible to everyone, and it would all have to be stored on storage media.

We chose Data Storage as our core and set about focusing our company on Data Storage, divesting our other businesses for value and driving cost reduction across all aspects of the company.

Imation's Core: Removable Data Storage Media

As you can imagine, a frenzy to back up data took place in the period leading up to the new millennium and the potential Y2K debacle which never took place. No wonder Data Storage's business dipped after the end of 1999. People had stocked up on our products. The technology problems we had faced earlier were solved in 2000 and

Data Storage came back into its own in 2001 and 2002.

The break-fix service business was the last business piece we sold and, while a few of our advisors favored closing this business immediately to gain the important focus we needed, we chose to have patience and sell it. We saved $40 million, and more important, we saved many jobs. This completed the realization of a strong focus on Data Storage.

Staffing Is the First Priority

The first thing we had to do was to staff Data Storage properly. Strong management was not in place, so we went outside to hire experienced people. Some of our outside hires brought great energy and discipline to the company. But, frankly, we made some mistakes. Some we hired had a dotcom mentality and turned out to be more interested in moving into "solutions" than in building our core business. Others did not value the long term employees who had built the Data business. A big culture clash within Data ensued. Suffice it to say Data Storage's success ended up being built on the work of courageous, experienced long-term Imation employees who knew the Data Storage business like Frank Russomano, Ron Zinke, Colleen Willhite, Subodh Kulkarni and their teams.

These dedicated people stayed the course during tough times and created success against stiff competition. The value of long experience in an industry should not be underestimated. We were fortunate to have data industry experts like those named above and also experienced leaders like

Larry Bode, Mark LeClair, Jim Ellis, Tom Lally, Jim Milligan and many others. We valued our 3M experience and leveraged it with change, urgency and financial discipline.

As we solidified our core—tape, diskettes, and optical disks—our returns improved. A focused company can concentrate all its efforts on building success, on using its strengths to win in the market, rather than constantly working to change the portfolio. Our customers could clearly understand who we were and what we could provide. We could now create real value for our shareholders and investors. We saved costs and cash by not making bets too far afield, and soon we were developing new growth around core areas that generated sustainable value. At last, we were focusing on our strengths and expanding on them. This led to exciting new programs like our Exabyte Tape investment, our purchase of EMTEC's tape assets and our distribution agreements with computer manufacturers. These tied well into our core competencies and generated profitable growth without new, unfamiliar investments in areas where we didn't have the experience or competency to win.

Exabyte is a good case in point of an acquisition that tied directly to our core. It made our tape franchise more valuable to our broad worldwide distribution. We decided it was worth it because our financial analysis showed we would earn solid margins, and our business analysis predicted Exabyte's new product opportunities would be well received in the market.

We didn't have to add any people. It made strong financial sense.

LESSONS LEARNED:

- A majority of successful businesses have achieved this status by growing their business around core competencies and core markets.
- Few companies have been successful long term by growing through acquisitions, especially when these do not relate closely to a company's core business.
- To find your core, identity your best customers, most differentiated capabilities, most critical products and important distribution channels. Match these with other strategic assets such as brand names and patents.
- Data Storage was our best bet because of our global market position, the projected growth of the industry, and our technology position.
- Look inside first for your leaders, people who know the business and the industry and have a personal commitment to the company.

Chapter Thirteen: The Value of Being Global

The importance of international business to success cannot be overemphasized. The world is now a small place, and business is accessible everywhere in the world. Opportunities are exploding. Without international business, our future would be very limited indeed. In addition, international business is exciting, profitable and the fastest growing opportunity available. To win, a company must set aside its U.S. market biases, and learn that the United States way is not always the right or best way to do business, which is why it's essential to become open to new ideas and different needs if your company is going to prosper in the global marketplace.

International Opportunities Are Huge!

At spin, almost fifty percent of our business was outside the United States. Now, International accounts for sixty-five percent. We are very bullish about this business, pursue all opportunities, and often go where our competition does not. After all, it's logical for truly global companies to have in excess of fifty percent of their business outside the U.S. when you think about it. About ninety-five percent of the world's population is non-U.S. and much more than fifty percent of business is done offshore. It's obvious business has much more room to grow outside our borders than it does inside. Not to take advantage of this would be to do your shareholders and employees a disservice.

What It Really Means to Be Global

Executives often think their company is global when it really is not. A company may sell worldwide and export product when possible, and even manufacture overseas, but that does not make it a global enterprise. Being truly global means addressing all opportunities equally, based on value and return, not "U.S. first and then we'll get to the rest." If opportunities are better in Asia or Latin America, a truly global company will put its priorities and assets there, and sacrifice elsewhere—even in its home country.

A global company needs a global focus. You must prioritize opportunities, investments and assets based on the financial return, regardless of what country they are in. An executive from International must sit in and take part in all key decisions at headquarters to assure non-U.S. opportunities are taken into consideration. A global company must report results globally by region (North America, Latin America, Europe, Asia, Eastern Europe) in order to evaluate progress in each region, and to assure all opportunities are addressed.

To be global, a company must have local people on the street in all key regions. This allows the company to know the customers, their languages and cultures, and to understand and meet their needs. After all, people buy from people, not organizations, and personal involvement is critical to sustainable success.

Global companies must also realize different regions of the world may call for different ways of organizing. European countries have close proximity so functions can often be centralized, and support personnel placed in only some of the countries, reducing redundant support costs. But in Asia, the distances are much greater, and each country needs to be more self-supporting.

In Latin America, currency is always an issue, so having Miami as headquarters and being a U.S. dollar-based business often makes sense. This is the system we have adopted for that part of the world. Even so, sales action must be in each country in the local language.

Executives in a global company visit international customers personally and often. How else can they acquire a full understanding of local needs and opportunities? Executives must understand the regional businesses, listen and learn so they can make the right decisions, and allocate resources correctly. They must know the customers, their needs, their cultural differences, and learn through firsthand experience. For example, Latin America is personal data storage oriented, but the U.S. is business storage driven.

We were fortunate when we spun off from 3M that my VP of International, Dave Wenck, and I knew a lot of people in International at 3M. As a result, we managed to take a number of the good ones with us. We knew who to pick and who to target in our negotiations with 3M. These key leaders built our international presence and a very solid, profitable business. People like Nobuyoshi Kawasaki in Japan and Asia, Dick Northup, Dave Ferraresi, Theo Bouwmans, Manuel Martinez, Paul Koglin, and Frank Hill in Europe, Raymond Yeong in China, J. W. Lee in Korea, Ron Hansen in Latin American and Doug Fraser in Canada. All of them and their teams had the real personal commitment to build an outstanding international business for Imation.

Our International Structure—"Think Global, Act Local"

Our businesses have what we call "country managers." At 3M they are called "managing directors." One of the things I changed after the spin was the way foreign subsidiaries were structured. 3M's policy was that no national from a country would lead a 3M unit in that country, so you never had a Belgian leading Belgium or a Frenchman leading the subsidiary in France. 3M had a reason for this. When these subsidiaries were originally created, nationals led each unit. As previously discussed, down-sizing in Europe is not prohibitive when it comes to the lower level people, but it is quite difficult when it comes to upper management. To jettison highly paid people costs a fortune—sometimes many times their annual pay plus other benefits.

It's no great mystery, then, why 3M had this policy. For example, when I first lived in Europe, working for 3M, there were actually two managing directors in one of the countries. One man was running the business, and the other sat at home drawing full pay. This was a far less expensive solution than firing him.

Difficulties had evolved for 3M because of nationals running the businesses, and they didn't want it to happen again. To avoid situations such as that, the pendulum had been allowed to swing all the way in the other direction. A European national could run a business in a European country, just not his own country. This led to a Spaniard running Japan, an American running Italy, and a Brit running Greece. But you never had a Brit running Britain.

We changed this because we were smaller and in a turnaround situation. We needed stronger customer focus. We put local nationals in charge in almost every country because they knew the language, the customs, and more important than anything, the customers. We have a Spaniard, Manuel Martinez, running Spain, a Dutchman, Theo Bouwmans, running Holland, and a German, Paul Koglin, running Germany, and so forth. These are basically sales organizations. Other functions for Europe report back to our European headquarters in Holland. We are organized to plan and manufacture globally but to act and serve customers locally. This provides jobs at home and creates sustainability.

The Asian Market

There are many different cultures and languages in Asia as well as strong borders and laws that make it difficult to move about and operate effectively without a fully-constituted local presence. The currencies all are different as are import and export laws. Moreover the distances between countries are great. This is why we have independent companies in each key country in Asia. Japan, China (Taiwan and Mainland), Korea, Singapore, and

Australia-New Zealand as each are unique.

Recently, we created an Asian leader, and each of the country managers now reports to him. They still have independence, but they report to one leader who in turn reports to the U.S. headquarters. These country managers in Asia run real businesses with IT, advertising, a balance sheet, debt, and they control their destiny. This is necessary because there is no easy way to consolidate. The distances are too great and there are daily export and government issues that must be dealt with.

Take China, as an amazing, exciting example. The first time I visited China was in the eighties. You had to have a lot of optimism and vision to see a positive future in China back then. Our 3M Director in China had his office in a hotel, and you had to climb over rubble to reach his door. But so much has changed in recent years.

Shanghai is now one of the most modern, efficient and beautiful cities in the world. It is a center of worldwide business and is fast taking its place next to the very top cities in the West. In 2008 the Olympics will be held in Beijing, and I expect change there will be incredible. They will gear up to make a huge impression, globally. The Olympics represent an enormous opportunity for China to build its reputation and leadership, and the Chinese will take advantage of it.

The European Market

Unlike Asia, the European market is not particularly spread out, nor is it as diverse. There are different languages and cultures to be sure, but most of the borders are open because of the European Common Market, and now, except for Great Britain, there is one main currency, the Euro. So a separate business in each country is simply not necessary. Instead, we have what basically amount to country sales organizations. We sell through distribution, so it's the job of our country teams to pull the products through. They call on data centers and manage the distribution, assuring users get what they need.

In short, the European country teams run the business on the street, which is critical to win, but we don't burden them with a lot of overhead. There's no need for a balance sheet. Support can be given on a consolidated basis. We want our European counterparts focused on selling, pricing, and on making money—not on running the entire breadth of a business. Some Europeans don't like this due to their desire to run their own show. But we've learned it's most beneficial for the focus to be on customers.

Building on 3M's Global Heritage

One of the most valuable things we learned from 3M was the importance of being a global corporation, of taking advantage of opportunities all over the world, and focusing on customers wherever they might be. As in all aspects of business, leaders must get out of their offices and touch, feel, and deal personally with customers in other countries if they are going to succeed to the fullest possible extent. One cannot run an international business remotely. That's why I visited our operations in every country at least once a year, and in Japan, Europe and China at least twice per year. My policy was that I had to meet with customers on every day of my visit. Our local people put my visits to good use, and we met hundreds and hundreds of customers. Customers are, after all, the reason we exist.

This policy put me in closer contact with the people who were using our products. It helped me understand them. It helped them understand us better, and to realize we cared. It also set an example for our local leaders and executives.

LESSONS LEARNED:

- Organize in a way that makes sense and is most efficient for each region of the world.
- Think and plan globally, but act locally.
- If your customers live all over the world, opportunities in all regions of the world must be evaluated with a level field based on R.O.I.
- Executives must meet customers face-to-face and know their needs.
- Local-language-speaking leaders are of critical importance. Be where the customer is, meet and understand his needs.
- Make the customer feel valued. Get executives out into the regions regularly to meet customers and carry your message to them, and to local employees.

Chapter Fourteen: What I Would Do Differently

A corporate culture is tough to change. It takes a long time, and it takes staying the course, yet being flexible when difficulties arise. At the beginning of Imation, I made the decision to go with an open office concept—no doors for anyone, including myself and our executives. The only exception was our legal staff, for obvious reasons.

While the open concept, overall, has worked well for eight years, fostering better communication and cooperation, the open office concept for executives failed. I was comfortable being in an open area with three of my reports, but it became clear not all of the executives were. We ran into problems in particular as we hired executives from the outside. After about eighteen months, we had cubicles created for executives. We went to small offices two years later. This experience helped teach us the value of change and of trying new approaches. It also brought home the necessity of continuing to change if certain moves aren't working.

We Oversold the Stock

Another error we made in the beginning was selling the stock too hard. As was written about earlier, we knew we were going to lose almost all our shareholders in the tax free spin off because it was clear most wouldn't want to hold

Imation in the long run. Over a period of a year or so we were pretty certain we would go through all the original shareholders. It's perhaps understandable we felt we needed to get out there and make the best pitch we could. But afterward, when Brad Allen, our Investor Relations Director and I sat down and talked about it, we agreed we'd sold our long term goals too hard and too well. We got people excited about the company at a time when we still had a lot of hard work and uexpected snags ahead of us. The stock came out at too high a price, and of course, it quickly corrected. The lesson is, when you're coming out, make sure to highlight the challenges as strongly as you highlight optimism and opportunities. That balance between challenges and opportunities is important so expectations do not become inflated. Otherwise, you're going to be struggling to keep investors in the boat as you go through the tough restructuring and difficult time that lies ahead. Take it from me, the job is more difficult when people's expectations are too high.

Our stock came out at twenty-four, went down to between twenty-one and twenty-two, and hung in that range for a while. Then, as we learned what we needed to change, we announced the restructuring. The stock dropped, and got as low as thirteen before we announced the sale of Medical Imaging to Kodak. We had created a hole to dig out of, and it took a few years of very consistent quarters to establish the value of our enterprise.

We Gave Too Many Employees Stock Options

I wanted our employees to feel real ownership in Imation. That led to giving stock options to everyone in the company. Our investors and Board supported the idea, but it turned out to be a mistake.

Everyone, including hourly workers, got at least a hundred stock option shares. This used up too many share options, and the value, or return, didn't materialize. Too large a disconnect exists between hourly workers and entry level people and our financial and value objectives. Most simply do not understand or appreciate the concept of options. My guess is it isn't immediate enough. Earlier, I told the story of having that come home to me when I was visiting our plant in West Virginia near Christmas in 1996. I realized at that moment stock options didn't mean anything to most of the people in that group. So we stopped the practice immediately, but not before we'd used many of our available options.

Nowadays at Imation you can still give options to anyone. As a manager, you get a certain number of shares to give to your people. You can award options to any one of your reports if it is justified by their performance. Anybody in the company can get options, but not automatically. I have a concern about the Sarbanes Oxley changes because now we must start expensing options. I'm not in favor of this. I'm in favor of putting tight restrictions on options for the top five people in a company, and even to expense these, because that's where the abuses have been and are likely to occur. As things now stand, the top people are still going to get options but having to expense them will reduce the number for rank and file who might gain great value from them.

A Check List of What to Do

We learned a great deal as we created our company—dealing with 3M's desires and barriers—and as we turned the company around into a financial success. The result is, if I had to do it over today, I would repeat many of our actions but also do a lot of things differently. What follows is a check list I hope will be of great value to you to help you achieve a turnaround.

- Conduct an immediate strategic analysis
- Question everything—all must make sense, financially
- Increase speed—drive urgency
- Sharpen focus on the core business faster
- Under promise and over deliver
- Your people determine the company's success. Value all, motivate them, challenge them.
- Rely on employees you already have on board if at all possible, i.e. experience in your business and industry.
- Don't talk reluctant employees into staying. Go with those committed to the challenge.
- Don't oversell future opportunities
- Cut the cord from the mother company even faster
- Target stock options carefully
- Put honesty and ethics first. They guide you well.

219

- Curb the enthusiasm of freedom. Force fundamentals and a step-by-step process.
- Realize you determine your value—not bankers.
- Business and financial fundamentals do not lie.
- Communicate, communicate, communicate.

No Regrets

People often ask me if I ever regret taking on the Imation challenge and leaving a solid, safe career at 3M. The answer is an unqualified no. The challenges we faced in turning around Imation were difficult for everyone in our company, as well as for our families. My wife gave up a lot while we worked with Imation—free time, vacations, more time together. Many other spouses and partners found themselves in similar situations. But the challenge was something I could never have passed up. It was the ultimate turnaround. A $2 billion start up, it was like jumping on a bucking bronco, rather than raising a facile colt. We were hands on, working in the trenches to survive and achieve success. I had the opportunity to face more issues that I ever would have at a start-up or a stable company. It was scary at times, but also very exciting and energizing.

When Imation's team finally came together, I had the privilege to be a part of a family. Imation has a courageous, dedicated team that is so necessary to compete in low margin, highly competitive businesses. It was an honor and a privilege to work with them through the dark times, and the exciting and good times.

LESSONS LEARNED:

- All new ideas in a change won't necessarily work. Be ready to alter those that don't. Do not be stubborn. Listen to the needs of your people.
- What works with some executives won't work with others, just as is the case with customers. Be flexible.
- Voice the challenges to your business. Under promise and over deliver.
- Don't hand out stock options to everyone. Be selective but broad based with company ownership.
- The biggest challenges in life provide the greatest sense of accomplishment when you meet them head on and rise to the task. Don't shy away. Go for it.

Epilogue

With Imation in a solid financial position and ready to build a bright future, I came to the conclusion my job with the company had been accomplished. It was a lot of hard work—exciting and fulfilling work to be sure—and I'd had tremendous support and help from many very capable people. Nonetheless, it was time to turn over the reins. So, in November 2003, I announced my retirement, and told the board I'd stay on through 2004 if necessary for a replacement to be found.

Imation Gets a New CEO, Bruce A. Henderson

After a thorough search, a new Chairman & CEO was identified, someone the Board and I felt strongly had the right credentials and background to lead Imation forward.

This gentleman is Bruce Henderson. He was offered the position, accepted it, and his appointment was announced in late spring of 2004. Bruce's strategic skills and experience are an ideal complement to the effective management team Imation now has in place. Bruce has a degree in electrical engineering and another in political science from Brown University, and he has an MBA from the Wharton School of Business of the University of Pennsylvania. He has been a management consultant with McKinsey and later ran several businesses for TRW, where as a supplier to

Toyota he learned the ins and outs of lean manufacturing and lean enterprise. More recently, Bruce was President and Chief Executive of Invensys Controls, a worldwide supplier of control systems for home and commercial HVAC systems and appliances. This was a high tech business with more than $3.5 billion in sales, 30,000-plus employees, and manufacturing plants in 16 countries. Perhaps as significant as this experience in terms of the direction Bruce is likely to take Imation, he is the author of what is perhaps the best-selling book of all time on how to make a company lean. The book is called *Lean Transformation: How to Turn Your Business into a Lean Enterprise*. More than 50,000 copies have been sold, a huge number considering its narrow appeal. Primarily this topic is of interest to top executives of companies in manufacturing. As sales of his book indicate, businesses all over the world are going lean nowadays in an effort to gain strategic advantages over their competition, and many are using *Lean Transformation* and its companion workbook as guides.

Just What Is a Lean Enterprise?

People who don't know about the lean movement and what it entails often jump to the conclusion it simply means doing more with less, and that this is accomplished simply by having everyone work harder. Nothing could be farther from the truth. More is done with less by having everyone work smarter. According to published data, people who work in true lean enterprises are significantly happier with their jobs on average than those who work in traditional businesses. Why? A fundamental reason is they are empowered to make decisions and get things done. In other words, they have more control over their jobs and their destinies.

Lean enterprises are distinguished by six key attributes: The workplace is safe, brightly lit, orderly, and immaculately clean. Products are produced on a just-in-time basis, only to customer demand (not to forecast). Products are made in continuous flow production lines which are scheduled according to customer demand, using pull-scheduling techniques.

The highest quality possible (Six Sigma) is built into products and processes, not inspected in. Equipment is programmed to detect defects, and operators will shut down a production line for quality reasons. Mistake proofing is used extensively. Root cause problem solving skills are finely honed.

Throughout an organization, teams of employees are empowered to make key decisions. Organizations are flat, with limited layers of management. Shop floor employees are cross-trained to perform multiple tasks and jobs.

In manufacturing facilities, visual management techniques are used extensively. Management is by sight, not only by computer.

In every department and area of a lean organization from the Chairman's office to the shipping department, there is relentless pursuit of waste reduction. "Simplify, simplify, simplify!" is the battle cry. Continuous improvement never ends in a lean enterprise. The core idea is that any and every activity or expense is to be eliminated that does not, in the view of the end user, add value to a product. This includes all functions and processes wherever they may be, not just unnecessary or redundant work on the factory floor. Elimination of inventory, for example, is especially critical since inventory tends to hide manufacturing and distribution bottlenecks that need to be identified and opened up. Moving goods, parts and components in and out of storage is considered a waste of time and money.

Lean enterprises enjoy a number of strategic advantages over their mass manufacturing competitors. First, a lean producer is typically the low-cost producer in its industry. This allows the lean enterprise to set the market price, as lean-producer Dell Computer has done in the PC world. Why? Lean manufacturing often requires half the space and 25 to 40 percent less direct labor cost than mass manufacturing. Inventory is often cut to two or three days supply, freeing up huge sums of money that would otherwise be tied up, along with enormous amounts of space previously required for storage. As you know, in the high tech arena, inventory that sits in a warehouse for any length of time before it is sold may end up being a worth a lot less than it was the day it was made. Imation found this out in 2004, as we will shortly discuss.

What else? Lean producers turn out high quality products. Because defects are virtually eliminated, customers are happy about the quality they receive. Next, back orders become a thing of the past. Lean producers make what a customer wants when he wants it, so users get what they want, and they get it fast.

This leads to what may be the biggest strategic advantage of lean—speed. Speed is the hallmark of a lean enterprise in several ways: speed of delivery of product that's configured as customers want it, speed with new product introductions, speed in management decision-making because the organization is flat and bureaucracy almost nonexistent. Speed can be a critical factor in success because a nimble organization unburdened by inventory can take full advantage of changes in the marketplace as they occur. Meanwhile, non-lean competitors will be scratching their heads, wondering what happened.

Bruce has already begun an initiative to transform Imation, which was already pretty lean when he arrived on board, into a true lean enterprise. I'm certain this transformation will make the company even stronger and more competitive in years to come.

Bruce and His Team Take on a Difficult Situation

Shortly after Bruce joined Imation, prices on optical products started falling. Although it was unforeseen at the time, a good deal of excess production capacity for these products existed in Asia, and manufacturers started flooding the market. This brought retail prices down by almost 60% on some products in a matter of weeks. Imation ended up having an inventory value problem, in technical terms "NRV" (Net Realizable Value), and had to write off $9 million at the end of the second quarter 2004. The result was the first "off" quarter in quite some time, which triggered a drop in the Imation stock price even though our magnetic tape business had performed well. The strong showing in magnetic tape during second quarter 2004 simply was not enough to make up for the huge drop in optical prices.

By third quarter 2004, prices of CDs and DVDs had begun to stabilize, the stock price had rebounded to $35, but the company nevertheless had been hurt because of the necessity of writing down the value of the inventory of those products. When prices drop as they did in this case, accounting rules allow writing down the value of inventory only to the price the company can reasonably expect to get for for that inventory. The result is that there is no profit margin remaining in this evaluation. When it is sold, it's sold essentially at break even. So, all the remaining inventory which had been written down had to be sold through at zero profit. On top of this, there was a weaker market for magnetic tape during that time. The result was two unfortunate quarters back to back, and the stock fell again to the low thirties before rebounding once again.

Restructuring Once More

To bring company costs in line with the new realities of lower optical prices and the increased competition in magnetic tape, Bruce and the management team undertook another restructuring of the company. This was announced at the end of the third quarter 2004 and implemented in about forty-five days. This was a painful but necessary realignment of costs with Imation's highly competitive marketplace.

Looking Ahead

At this writing, Imation has had two solid quarters financially (Q404 and Q105) and is back on its feet with strong financial and operational performance. The Imation team has begun the process of developing the vision for the next phase of the company's evolution. The magnetic tape business is robust and its optical market is strenghtening. In addition, Imation has an extremely strong balance sheet with $400 million in cash and no debt. This suggests strategic acquisitions are a possibility. In examining this direction, the analysis will surely include another close look at Imation's core competencies. When one considers the nature of Imation's products, it's evident the company has a very solid scientific capability as well as strong intellectual property. It's a fact the company is unsurpassed at fundamental chemistry, physics and materials science. Imation is also excellent at manufacturing, particularly the manufacture of thin film, and is able to take a substrate such as polyester or polycarbonate and coat it with an extremely precise set of layers of media that allow optical or magnetic recording. Only three companies in the world can do this: Imation, Fuji and Maxell.

THE STORY I HAVE to write of Imation and its turnaround comes to a close in mid 2005. The ground work has been set. Imation now has a new, lower cost base that's in line with the marketplace in which it now must operate.

The company is in a strong position to move forward in what has become an industry that's even more competitive than it was in 1996 when we began. The balance sheet is strong and solid. Potential directions and strategies for the future are in the works and being explored. The future looks bright both for the short term and for the long term.

I wish Bruce and Frank and all my friends at Imation the very best of everything and leave them knowing the company is in good hands. I will watch with interest to see what moves they make.

Good luck and *Bon Voyage!*

Imation Has Established a Solid Platform for Sustainable Profitable Growth

Focus on Data Storage and Accelerate Growth

Rationalize the Portfolio

Restructure and Stabilize the Business

Spin-off and Create New Company

1996 1997 1998 1999 2000 2001 2002 2003 2004

APPENDIX
Profiles of 3M Business
That Were Spun Off

Data Storage

MISSION:

To build and enhance worldwide leadership position in branded removable data storage media solutions and applications for Desktop, Network (midrange) and Enterprise (data center) system environments.

CUSTOMERS:

PC users at all levels of computing sophistication • LAN/network administrators • Data center managers

MARKET TRENDS:

Move from commodity to semi-proprietary solutions • Growth of high-capacity network and multi-user storage requirements, versus stand-alone desktop storage • Increased storage requirements, driven by increasing image/color content and Internet/network applications

MAJOR PRODUCTS:

SuperDisk™ 120MB diskettes the 3.5-inch, high-capacity next generation storage diskette • Travan NS data cartridges • SLR/MLR data cartridges • 3480, 3490E, 3590 data cartridges • Travan data cartridges • 1.44MB diskettes

SOLUTIONS FOCUS:

High-capacity, networked multi-media storage solutions Hardware/software/ media/services)• Leverage data storage expertise to meet the needs of medical imaging and printing & publishing customer • Media asset management • Worldwide service/support

Printing and Publishing

MISSION:

To be the preferred supplier of innovative products, services, digital/brand asset management and workflow solutions for printing and publishing applications.

CUSTOMERS:

Publications • Commercial printers • Quick printers • In-plant printers • Trade shops • Ad agencies • Ad/print specifiers • Packaging market • Corporate Customers

MARKET TRENDS:

Moving trend from conventional to digital printing applications • Demand for total workflow integration and management • Migration to digital workflow • Color management • Media asset management • Dry film/plates • Brand asset management solutions • Time/cost reduction increasing as competitive differentiator • Demand for environmentally friendly systems

MAJOR PRODUCTS:

Digital color proofing systems (Rainbow™) • Conventional color proofing systems (Matchprint® Color-Key™) • Graphic arts plates (No-Process) • Graphic arts • Workflow automation and data communication software • Matchprint Laser Proof • Spectral Profiler color tools • Imation publishing software • Media asset management • Brand asset management • Device independent color management tools • Complete line of high quality carbonless paper, pre-perfed bond and other specialized products for both offset and electronic printing applications

SOLUTIONS FOCUS:

Leverage color science, color management expertise across conventional and digital workflows • Leverage dry technology expertise • Leverage data storage expertise • Worldwide service/support • Leverage color science expertise • Leverage workflow expertise • Maintain product quality and customer loyalty, while managing business for maximum efficiency

Medical Imaging

MISSION:

Expand leadership position in hard copy recording and provide integrated imaging and information management solutions for medical diagnostics and PACS for Printing, Viewing, Archiving, Acquisition, Conventional imaging, Teleradiology

CUSTOMERS:

Hospital radiology departments • Government • National hospital buying groups • Mobile imaging companies • Imaging centers

MARKET TRENDS:

Chemistry-free systems (DryView™) • Standards-based electronic imaging software • Digital image capture • Electronic management of medical images • Demand for environmentally friendly systems • PACS • Teleradiology

MAJOR PRODUCTS:

Electronic laser recording systems (hardware, interfaces and accessories) • DryView (line)
- 8700 industry standard (14x17)
- 8600 Mammography (8x10)
- 8300 Desktop (8x10)
- 8100 (Single input 14x17)
-8500 (11x14)

• Image management systems (software and storage media) • AutoRad • ArchiveManager™ • TeleMax™ • ClinicalAccess™ • Conventional x-ray products

SOLUTIONS FOCUS:

Integrate DryView products with image~e management network solutions • PACS• Leverage data storage expertise• Worldwide service/support

Photo Color

MISSION:

Maintain position as the leading supplier of private label color print film to retailers.

CUSTOMERS:

Mass-market discounters • Chain drug stores • Grocery store chains • Mail-order photo finishers

MARKET TRENDS:

Growing digital photography segment • Growing% digital management of photographic images

MAJOR PRODUCTS:

New, user-friendly film format (APS) • Complete line of HP ~films (100, 200, 400) • 35mm color HP print films (100, 200, 400) • 35mm color slide films (100, 400, 640T)• Single-use cameras • Photo quality inkjet paper • Consumer and technical support

SOLUTIONS FOCUS:

Global focus on the private label market segment • Leverage storage capabilities to support growing digital photography storage

Customer Solutions Service

MISSION:
Provide high quality, timely support, maintenance and optimization of Imation products and technology platforms.

CUSTOMERS
Imation's worldwide service organization delivers unsurpassed service to Imation customers in more than 60 countries. Field service engineers provide on-site solutions and customer service personnel provide around-the-clock telephone assistance.

MARKET TRENDS:
Transition to digital technologies and broad-based workflow solutions requiring greater focus on software and network service and support

MAJOR PRODUCTS:
Offers professional services:
- Services consulting
- Operations management
- Training
Technical documentation• Global Field Services offers support with over 1,200 service engineers • Global Support Centers provide 24-hour customer assistance through over 100 toll-free phone lines • Global Parts Service Centers ensure timely and accurate delivery of service parts • More than 2,000 customer contacts per day

SOLUTIONS FOCUS:

Integrated global support for imaging and information platforms, media, software and workflow environments to users of Imation products

Document Imaging

MISSION:

Maintain contribution of mature business.

CUSTOMERS:

Large, diverse end-user base including manufacturers, engineering firms and government organizations requiring records retention, design document and industrial imaging back-up.

MARKET TRENDS:

Ongoing transition to digital/electronic document storage replacing traditional paper/film processes

MAJOR PRODUCTS:

Turn-key systems to meet office and engineering document management needs • Printers that deliver large format engineering drawing prints directly from digital databases.

SOLUTIONS FOCUS:

Maintain product quality and customer loyalty, while managing business for maximum efficiency

Index

Lexmark, 37, 121
Lidstad, Dick, 36
Lincoln, Abraham, 51, 70
Lombardi, Vince, 70, 73

Maarek, Armand, 135
Mann, Marvin, 37, 121
managing directors, 210
Matchprint®, 40, 96, 162-163, 177, 235
Martinez, Manuel, 209, 211
Matthews, White, 122
Maxell, 32, 80, 229
McKesson, 121
McKinsey & Co, 223
McNamara, Jack, 137, 154
McQuade, Mike, 187
Medical Imaging, 18, 29, 30, 42, 96, 116, 177, 182-183, 186, 188, 203, 217, 234
Medtronic, 69, 121, 144
Melchoir, Barry, 35, 137
metal particulate, 163
metaphysician, 48
Microsoft, 122
Milligan, Jim, 205
Minnesota Timberwolves, 122
Mitsubishi, 80
Mnookin, Professor Robert, 167
Mosaic, 33
Moser Baer, 167, 179-180
Myers-Briggs, 63

Neidermire, John, 135, 154

Nelson, Ron, 35
Northup, Richard, 77
Newco, 19, 25, 49, 95
NRV (Net Realizable Value), 227

Oakdale, 35, 45, 96, 109, 228
Olympics, 212
On Death and Dying, 49
optical market, 228
Oracle, 154-155

Patton, General George, 70
Pennsylvania, University of, 223
Phillips, Joe, 188
Photo Color, 239
Photo Film, 18, 30, 42
Power of Believing, The, 47
Power of Positive Thinking, The, 47
Profit from the Core, 199-202
Public Radio, 28, 96
Pulido, Mark, 121
pull-scheduling, 224

Rastogi, Sharad, 188
Reagan, Ronald, 47, 72
Reich, Charles, 122
Retenwald, Debra, 154
Rigby, Darrell, 188
Roosevelt, Franklin Delano, 71
Russomano, Frank, 58, 59, 171, 204, 223